THE BIBLICAL ACCOUNT OF

THE CONQUEST OF CANAAN

THE BIBLICAL ACCOUNT

OF THE

CONQUEST OF CANAAN

by

YEHEZKEL KAUFMANN

With a Preface to the Reissue
by

MOSHE GREENBERG

JERUSALEM

THE MAGNES PRESS, THE HEBREW UNIVERSITY

Translated into English by

M. DAGUT

Distributed by The Magnes Press,
The Hebrew University, Jerusalem 91904, Israel

First edition, 1953
Second edition, 1985

©

By The Magnes Press
The Hebrew University
Jerusalem 1985

Printed in Israel
ISBN 965–223–556–3

CONTENTS

Maps

ABBREVIATIONS

Alt, Israels Gaue	A. Alt, Israels Gaue unter Salomo, Alttestamentliche Studien R. Kittel zum 60. Geburtstag dargebracht, 1913, pp. 1—19.
Alt, Judas Gaue	A. Alt, Judas Gaue unter Josia, PJB, 1925, pp. 100—117.
Alt, Landnahme	A. Alt, Die Landnahme der Israeliten in Palästina, 1925.
Alt, Stammesgrenzen	A. Alt, Das System der Stammesgrenzen im Buche Josua, Sellin-Festschrift, 1927, pp. 13—24.
Alt, Ortsliste	A. Alt, Eine galiläische ortsliste in Jos. 19, ZAW, 1927, pp. 59—81.
Alt, Josua	A. Alt, Josua, Werden und Wesen des A. T., Beihefte zur ZAW, 1936, pp. 13—29.
Elliger, ZDPV 1930	K. Elliger, Die Grenze zwischen Ephraim und Manasse, ZDPV, 1930, pp. 265—309.
Elliger, PJB 1934	K. Elliger, Josua in Judäa, PJB, 1934, pp. 47—71.
Gressman, Anfänge	H. Gressmann, Die Anfänge Israels. Die Schriften des A. T., I$_2$, 1914.
Mowinckel, Josua 13-19	S. Mowinckel, Zur Frage nach dokumentarischen Quellen in Josua 13—19, 1946.
Noth, ZDPV 1935	M. Noth, Studien zu den historisch-geographischen Dokumenten des Josuabuches, ZDPV, 1935, pp. 185—255.
Noth, Josua (also Comm. to Josh)	M. Noth, Das Buch Josua, Handbuch zum A. T., ed. Eissfeldt, 1938.
Rudolph, Elohist	W. Rudolph, Der "Elohist" von Exodus bis Josua, Beihefte zur ZAW, 1938.
Simons, Structure	J. Simons, The Structure and Interpretation of Josh. XVI—XVII, Orientalia Nederlandica, 1948, pp. 190—215.
Steuernagel, Josua	C. Steuernagel, Das Buch Josua, Handkommentar zum A. T., ed. Nowack, 1899.
Wright, Problem	G. E. Wright, The Literary and Historical Problem of Joshua 10 and Judges 1, Journal of Near Eastern Studies, 1946, pp. 105—114.

A. T. — Altes Testament. PJB — Palästinajahrbuch. ZAW — Zeitschrift für die alttestamentliche Wissenschaft. ZDPV — Zeitschrift des deutschen Palästina-Vereins.

Gen — Genesis. Ex — Exodus. Lev — Leviticus. Nu — Numbers. Deut — Deuteronomy. Josh — Joshua. Ju — Judges. Sam — Samuel. Ki — Kings. Is — Isaish. Jer — Jeremiah. Ez — Ezekiel. Am — Amos. Ob — Obadiah. Hab — Habakkuk. Zech — Zechariah. Ps — Psalms. Ezr — Ezra. Neh — Nehemiah. Chr — Chronicles.

PREFACE TO THE REISSUE

by

MOSHE GREENBERG

Yehezkel Kaufmann (1889–1963) is the towering figure in modern Jewish Bible scholarship. He came to the study of the Bible by way of a broad inquiry into Jewish history – embodied in his masterly four-volume *Gola ve-nekhar* ("Exile and Alienation"), completed in 1929. Kaufmann's lifelong goal was to identify the essential motives of Jewish history. A believer in the power of ideas to shape societies and events, he regarded as the key factor in that history the strong bond of nationality and religion. To understand that bond Kaufmann reached back ever further until he arrived at its origin – the biblical period, to the investigation of which he dedicated the rest of his life. His major opus, *Toldot ha-emuna ha-yisreelit* ("A History of Israelite Religion") was planned to cover the subject (as its subtitle read) "from its beginnings to the end of the Second Temple period." The first volume appeared in 1937; by 1956 seven more had been published, bringing the study down to early Second Temple times, when the Jews were under Persian domination. But by then an unlooked-for change of purpose had occurred in Kaufmann: instead of proceeding to the Hellenistic age of Judaism he turned back to the books of Joshua and Judges – the start of Israel's history in its land. In 1953 the presently reprinted monograph was published – the first considerable work of Kaufmann to appear in English; this preliminary study gave notice of his altered direction. A full-dress commentary to the book of Joshua, detailing the exegetical underpinnings of the monograph, followed in 1959. Kaufmann's "public" hoped that now his preoccupation with that subject would be exhausted, and that he would resume his "History". But as soon as he finished commenting Joshua he began his commentary on the book of Judges – an approach to which he had suggested in the present monograph (that commentary was published in 1962).

9

Preface

I was at that time an instructor at the University of Pennsylvania, an admirer of Kaufmann from a distance. My youthfully rash project of translating and abridging the first seven volumes of the "History" had just appeared (as *The Religion of Israel, from its Beginnings to the Babylonian Exile*, Chicago: University of Chicago, 1960; later a Schocken paperback) and I awaited continuation of the "History" in order to finish my task. Kaufmann answered my anxious query about his plans in a letter of 17 Sivan 5720 (12 June 1960):

> I am presently working on the Song of Deborah. I see that you too are not happy with my absorption in the exposition of these books. Your opinion is, to tell the truth, that of all my friends; but I cannot agree. I do not plan to comment on all of the Former Prophets, but the case of Joshua and Judges is special: these books relate the *beginnings* of the people of Israel, and their testimony is decisive also for the beginnings of the *religion* of Israel. Prevailing criticism labors at demolishing these monuments. Here are historical narratives prior to the monarchy, and this [fact] criticism will not acknowledge in any way, because to do so would demolish its edifice. For such a complicated problem general explanations are of no avail. One must deal with every chapter, every verse. Eissfeldt, in his review of my monograph on Joshua [the presently reprinted work, which E. reviewed in "Die Eroberung Palästinas durch Altisrael," *Die Welt des Orients* 2 (1955), 158–171] wondered at my not having anything to say about Judg 3:2, and considered that a major stricture. Had I dealt with that verse challenges would have been raised about other verses. One must produce a detailed commentary, and I am only sorry that I cannot find someone to translate [mine on] Joshua.

Kaufmann's two commentaries (modern continuations of the great medieval tradition of Jewish philological exegesis) have still not been translated, nor is there at present a prospect that they will be. It is therefore appropriate that after the lapse of decades his preliminary study in English of the literary-historical problems of these books, and his critique of views that are still considered basic for modern study of them be once again made available.

The lasting value of this monograph is in its advocacy of an alternative to the still prevalent critical opinion that much of the material in the biblical conquest stories comes from late monarchic times and hardly reflects the actual course of events. This opinion is admittedly a hypothesis, and "By definition such a hypothesis is devised to explain most completely what we *now* know, *not* what it may be necessary or possible for another generation to say" (G.E. Wright, *Joshua*, Anchor Bible, Garden City: Doubleday, 1982, p. 78). Moreover, acceptance of any hypothesis is a matter of judgment based on presuppositions whose permanency is by no means assured (see ibid. p. 72). For the good of scholarship it is necessary to maintain awareness of the hypothetical nature of current judgments, and no better means of doing so exists than the presentation of contrary arguments. When such are advanced by a scholar of Kaufmann's stature, the obligation to scholarship of seeing to the continued availability of his work is clear.

Western scholars received Kaufmann's monograph with respect but demurred at his conclusions (Rowley, *Bibliotheca Orientalis* 11 [1954] 227f.; Wright, *Journal of Biblical Literature* 75 [1956] 154f.; Bright, *Early Israel in Recent History Writing*, Chicago: Allenson, pp. 56–78). Kaufmann's distaste for speculation on the tradition-history of the literature in question put him outside the circle of western discussants, who have always set great store by such speculation. I consider most questionable his leap from literary criticism to historical reconstruction. What he has shown is that the Bible describes a possible course of conquest – when read with allowances for its legendary and literary features. But to proceed from there to asserting its servicibility for reconstructing history is more difficult than Kaufmann would seem to admit. He takes practically no account of archeological data (his commentries correct that lack only slightly); but these are ever increasing and ever more complicated and must be integrated with the literary record by the historian. Moreover, the plausibility of a course of events can hardly be judged (as Kaufmann seems to judge it) in isolation from the socio-economic framework to which it belonged.

It is, finally, necessary to say a word about the style of this monograph. Kaufmann's stake in his conclusions is manifest not only in the passage from his letter cited above, but throughout his writing; he did not hide his sentiments and his evaluations from the reader's view. This is not the usual practice in English scholarly writing. I recall my chagrin at the faithfulness of Dagut's translation of this monograph: what a pity, I thought, that the first introduction of Kaufmann to the English-reading world conveys so ingenuously his typically scholastic style of free-swinging polemic. (In my abridgment of the "History" I took pains to filter out most of the strong language.) The English reader must make allowance for this stylistic gap and focus on the argument, not on the imputations and impugnings that accompany it (see Bright's strictures, p. 71, fn. 1; McKenzie, *Catholic Biblical Quarterly* 17 [1955] 95).

After all is said, Bright's judgment of the virtues of this monograph remains valid: "A healthy corrective and a refreshing contrast to overmuch nihilism [with respect to the story of the conquest. It contains] a host of details penetrating in the extreme... stimulating because the author possesses a keen argumentative mind, is fully conversant with the material, and approaches it from an entirely novel point of view; a combination that is bound to produce fresh insights" (p. 67f.)

The Hebrew original of this monograph (*Ha-sippur ha-miqra'i al kibbush ha-arets*) was published in Jerusalem by Mosad Bialik in 5715 (1955). In this reprint we have appended seven maps following the Hebrew edition, adapted by Shmuel Aḥituv.

M.G.

Jerusalem, Pesaḥ 5744 (April 1984)

THE FORMER PROPHETS AND THE SOURCES
OF THE PENTATEUCH

It is generally accepted that the historical books of the Bible
have come down to us in a late recension made in the spirit of
the Pentateuchal Schools. This view applies particularly to the
Books of Joshua and Judges. According to it, these books, in
their extant form, contain no *original and authentic information*
about the conquest of Palestine and the period of the Judges,
apart from the Song of Deborah. The stories and records are
not contemporary with the events, but comprise material which
was given shape in later times. This view is supported by various
arguments. First, Josh and Ju contain literary elements which
are related in style and subject-matter *to the sources of the Pentateuch*. In Josh we find Deuteronomistic passages, as also passages
which belong to P. In both books the Deuteronomistic redaction
is allegedly discernible. Moreover, the pragmatical framework of Ju
would appear to be Deuteronomistic. Here then is proof, according
to the usual assumptions of Biblical criticism, that the books were
edited at the end of the 7th Century and at the beginning of the Second Temple. Secondly, the Higher Criticism believes to have revealed a fundamental contradiction between the stories of the Conquest in Josh and in Ju 1 respectively. According to Josh the whole
country was conquered in a full-scale national war and divided
amongst the tribes in Joshua's lifetime; whereas, according to Ju 1
only a part of the country was conquered, and that in separate
tribal wars. This latter version is considered earlier and more historical than the version given in Josh. However, Ju 1 is also
thought to be a late synthesis of traditional material from the
period of the early Kingdom, or later still. Thirdly, there is an

established opinion that the stories in Josh 1-11 and in Ju were, in their original form, local and tribal stories which have been converted into national sagas by later redaction. Israel did not exist as a single, united nation before the Kingdom. What existed before the Kingdom was, at the very most, an "amphictyonic" tribal league, and even this may not have included all the tribes. Alt, Noth and their followers made special efforts to prove that the stories in Josh were originally no more than local aetiological legends of the tribe of Benjamin originating in the tribal sanctuary at Gilgal.

In recent years, most scholars have given up the attempt to find in Josh (and in the other Former Prophets) a continuation of the Pentateuchal sources (J, E, D, P). Nor has *Rudolph's* effort to prove that the nucleus of the story in Josh is the continuation of J won conviction. It has been recognized that Josh is an independent work. Alt, Noth, Albright and others find in Josh source material of various date which is not connected with the Pentateuch sources. Wright, moreover, has even challenged the accepted evaluation of Josh as against Ju 1 [1]. He maintains that the contradiction between Ju 1 and Josh 1-11 is not as great as the scholars of the last generation argued. In addition, he tries to prove that Ju 1 is a congeries of variegated fragments differing in date and trustworthiness, and that there is no ground for the assumption that it is more historical than Josh 1-11. On the basis of archaeological and topographical material, he shows that the description of the war in Josh 10 is grounded in strategic reality.

In spite of this, it cannot be said that in the field of Biblical science any fundamental change has taken place either in the general critical attitude, or in the specific historical evaluation of Josh and Ju. Scholars follow the well-trodden paths and continue the "tradition". They base their examination of the Biblical text on the rules of Latin composition. They start from the assumption that the true and original text must be "consistent"; if it is not "consistent", it must be corrected by scissors and

1) Wright, Problem.

14

paste work. The Biblical story-teller must have a "schema"; he must keep to a "sequence"; he is not allowed to repeat himself; he is forbidden to retrace his steps etc. Scholars discover everywhere duplications, contradictions, derangements of sequence etc., and "emend". According to them, the text has been tampered with by the first, second, and third hands of "redactors" and "expanders", most of whom were complete fools and botchers. It does not occur to scholars that the Biblical author wrote in an entirely different way, and not according to the schema of a Latin composition. Hence we should welcome the protest of Widengren and his colleagues against what Widengren calls "debaucheries of literary criticism" and against the assumption that the text was worked over by "the silliest asses" who had not the faintest understading of it [2]. However, the adversaries of the Literary Criticism are prone to make the mistake of throwing out the baby with the bath-water: to reject *literary criticism as such*, instead of rejecting only the faulty and ridiculous *application* of this criticism by scholars. But their protest, as such, is just. It must be added, however, that the abandonment of the search for continuations of the Pentateuch sources in the historical books, so far from improving the state of research into these books, has actually made it much worse. The source is, after all, something concrete and fixed as regards style and subject-matter, and therefore the search for "sources" was based on some objective factor, or, at least, constituted an attempt to achieve a certain degree of objectivity. Whereas now even this no longer exists. Now anyone can analyse, erase, alter etc., from considerations which are purely subjective, and on the dogmatic assumptions of some personal theory which the text must be made to fit. This represents a deterioration even from the previous level.

Moreover, giving up the search for a continuation of the Pentateuchal sources in the historical books could not of itself produce a fundamentally new valuation of Josh and Ju. For, one fact at least is beyond dispute: that these books contain elements bearing

2) Widengren, Literary and Psychological Aspects of the Hebrew Prophets, 1948, pp. 82-83.

the stamp of P and D. Hence the dating of P and D automatically fixes the date when Josh and Ju were composed or edited. In particular, there has been no modification of the view that, the Former Prophets are "a Deuteronomistic historical work" whether the product of editors belonging to the Deuteronomistic school, or of a single historian who set the Deuteronomistic imprint upon the whole tradition. If this is the case, it follows that the date of the composition of Josh and Ju cannot be placed earlier than the end of the 7th Century.

I have elsewhere[3] brought numerous detailed proofs to show that P is *older* than D and contains early, archaic material. It will subsequently be seen that Josh 21 (belonging to P) is extremely archaic, — earlier than the period of the Judges. On this assumption, the priestly elements in Josh do not fix a late date for the book. However, I admit that the extant book of Deut belongs to the time of *Josiah*, viz: the end of the 7th Century. Therefore, I must consider the question whether the dating of the Josianic Deut also fixes the date of the composition of Josh and Ju.

---

3) In my article in ZAW, 1930, and especially in my book תולדות האמונה הישראלית Vol. 1.

THE FORMER PROPHETS ARE NOT "A DEUTERONOMISTIC HISTORICAL WORK"

The claim that the Former Prophets are "a Deuteronomistic historical work" is ambiguous and misleading. It has long been recognized that there is an *early nucleus* in Deut and that only the legislation about the *unification of the cult* can be assigned to the 7th Century, in the time of Josiah (or Hezekiah-Josiah). Even the Law Code in cc. 12-26 contains laws and groups of laws which have nothing to do with the unification of the cult and the period of Josiah. Above all, it should be stressed that, in the chapters which form the framework of the book (1-11, 27-36), the commandment of the unification of the cult is not once mentioned. Hence the whole historical philosophy of Deut has no original connection with the idea of the unification of the cult and is older than it. Typical of the unifying legislation (or of the "Josianic" stratum) of Deut is the prohibition against offering sacrifice "in any place" (on the *bamoth*), and the commandment to sacrifice only at a single chosen place where a whole series of cultic duties are to be performed. The distinguishing stylistic mark of this legislation is "the place which He shall choose". The epithet "Deuteronomistic" is therefore ambiguous: it describes a relation to both the early D and the later (Josianic) D. If it is said that the Former Prophets are "a Deuteronomistic historical work", we must further ask: In the early or late sense? For the stamp "Deuteronomistic" does not of itself fix the date of a literary work as the 7th Century.

Now it is a fact that in the Former Prophets the idea of the unification of the cult appears *only* from 1 Ki 3 2 onwards. Before this there is no mention of it. There is a contact in style and

subject-matter with Deut, but — only with the early Deut, more
precisely — only with the chapters forming the framework in which
the unification of the cult is not mentioned at all. It is true that
scholars have found the unifying conception in several passages
before 1 Ki 3, but only by resorting to artificial exegesis. The
truth is that the conception finds no expression even in the
passages where it would most naturally be expected. Thus, according to Josh 21 42 22 4 23 1 the conditions of Deut 12 9-10 had
already been fulfilled in Joshua's lifetime: God had given Israel
rest from all the enemies round about them. But Joshua does
not build a Chosen House, nor does he give orders for it to be
built in the future. 1 Sam 2 27-36 is concerned with a *central
sanctuary*, not a single Chosen House, since the background of
the prophecy is the position of the House of Eli at *Shiloh* which
was not a single Chosen House in the sense of Deut. In 2 Sam 7 1
the condition of Deut 12 9-10 is again mentioned. But this chapter
deals with the building not of a single Chosen House, but of
"a house of cedar-wood" for *the Ark*, a feature which is nowhere
mentioned in the legislation of Deut about the unification of
the cult. Even in the story about the erection of the altar on
the threshing floor of Araunah (2 Sam 24), there is no mention
of building a Chosen House. It is only necessary to compare
this story with its setting in 1 Chr 21 to see that the Book
of Samuel has not been subjected to any Deuteronomistic redaction. The Chosen Place is mentioned only in Josh 9 27 in
these words: "to the place which He shall choose". But it has
already been recognized that these words, coming at the end of
the chapter after its proper conclusion, are a late addition [4]. These
words are the only manifestation of the Josianic-Deuteronomistic

---

4) The addition is still more obvious in the Septuagint version where the
rendering reads: "and unto the place which He shall choose". Moreover, these
words are preceded by an additional verse not found in the Hebrew. Noth,
Joshua, p. XIII, is of the opinion that the story about the building of the altar
on Mount Ebal in Josh 8 35-30 refers to the fulfilment of D's ordinance about
the unification of the site of the cult i. e. in Shechem, which was thus at
first regarded as "the place that Jahweh will choose". But there is no mention

"redaction" of Josh 1-1 Ki 2. It follows that the Deuteronomistic element in Josh and Ju is early and has no connection with the 7th Century.

Again, the Deuteronomistic idea of the unification of the cult is not mentioned in the priestly chapters of Josh either. I have elsewhere endeavoured to show that P nowhere mentions D's unification of the cult. The conception of a single chosen *place* is not referred to in P. Likewise, all those special laws which in D are connected with the unification of the cult in one chosen place are lacking in P. The Tent of Assembly in P is a portable sanctuary which has nothing in common with the Chosen Place of D. In P the high-places (bamoth) are not proscribed. Lev 17 merely forbids sacrifice "in the field", without a shrine. This opposition to field sacrifices also forms the background of Josh 22 (vide infra). But P does not proscribe the shrines: on the contrary, the cultic code of P is to be regarded as a code regulating worship on the *bamoth* of which the Tent of Meeting is the prototype. — Thus even the Priestly elements in Josh do not date the book in the seventh century or later.

This fundamental difference which we find between the Books of Kings and Josh — Ju — Sam proves that the Former Prophets are not to be regarded as a *uniform* work resulting from the uniform compilatory or editorial activity of either a school or a single historian. The late Deuteronomistic recension of the Books of Kings proves that they were compiled after the period of Josiah, while the absence of such a recension in the three previous books shows that they belong to an earlier date. However, neither are these three books a uniform work, nor were they all compiled at the same time. Their literary character marks them as entirely distinct from each other. Sam is unique in that it does not contain *a single passage* (not even in its pragmatic framework) written in the Deuteronomistic style. The passages which Budde and his followers consider "undoubtedly", or al-

---

at all of Shechem in the story, nor is there any allusion to its being chosen as the one and only cultic site. The celebration on Mount Ebal was held only once.

most undoubtedly, Deuteronomistic (1 Sam 2$_{27-36}$ 8 10$_{17-26}$ 12 2 Sam 7) contain nothing at all of the style of D. Moreover, in 1 Sam 8 the kingship is a sin, but not in Deut 17$_{17-20}$; nor is there in Deut any reference to the "Regulation of the Kingship" which appears in 1 Sam 8. Even in 1 Sam 12 there is no mention of the instruction given to the king in Deut 17 $_{16-20}$. Similarly, the Books of Sam do not contain a single fragment of P. It is otherwise with Josh and Ju, which have stylistic contacts with D and P. But obviously this affinity cannot be used to prove that they are a homogeneous work or that they have both undergone a common recension. Josh is a unique literary entity which in subject-matter rounds off the story of the Pentateuch.

Still less is there any ground for attaching portions of the Pentateuch to the Former Prophets and regarding them as a single document. Deut too never belonged to such a work, as Noth attempts to prove [5]. We have already seen that the Josianic Deut influenced only the recension of Kings, while there is no special connection between the early Deut and the Former Prophets as a whole. The ideas which appear in both of them (the choice of Israel, the conception of the Covenant, punishment for rebellion etc.) [6], being common to all the sources of the Pentateuch, do not indicate any special relation to Deut.

The fact that Josh and Ju contain verses and passages written in the style of D (and P) is not necessarily to be interpreted as a sign of a school's or an individual's *dependence* on the literature of the Pentateuch. It proves no more than that Josh and Ju included material from the work of authors who wrote in the style of the Pentateuch, especially in the style of D. Presumably ancient Israel boasted a rich literature written in these styles which has not come down to us. Certainly, affinity with the literature of the Pentateuch cannot decide the question of the date of the composition of Josh and Ju. This date is to be fixed by the *internal evidence*, without any preconceived notions.

5) Noth, Überlieferungsgeschichtliche Studien, I, 1943.
6) Noth, ibid. pp. 100 sqq.

THE ARCHAIC CHARACTER OF THE BOOK
OF THE DISTRIBUTION OF THE LAND (JOSH 13-19)

A straightforward examination of Josh reveals that the *latest* event explicitly mentioned in it is the conquest of Leshem (Laish) by the Danites (19 47). This is a hard fact, and all the attempts of scholars, by means of artificial exegesis, to find later material to suit preconceived theories will not bear critical investigation.

In Josh 13-19, the Book of the Distribution of the Land, we find descriptions of the inheritances of the tribes on both sides of the Jordan. These descriptions do not all bear the same stamp, but fall into various categories. For Judah and Benjamin (15, 18) we are given detailed boundary lists and detailed lists of cities. In the case of Ephraim (16) the southern border is given in detail, as is the border of Ephraim-Manasseh, whereas the northern border of Manasseh is described in general terms (17 10-11). The cities of Ephraim and Manasseh are not mentioned at all. For Simeon (19) there is only a list of cities. For Dan too (ibid.) there is perhaps only a list of cities. Of the northern territory of Dan no description at all is given. When we come to the Galilean tribes (ibid.) we find a rather confused and fragmentary mixture of lists of boundaries and lists of cities. It is evident that there are omissions in these lists. A similar mixture of cities and boundaries occurs in the case of Reuben and Gad (13), nor are the boundaries described in detail. The territory of half Manasseh (ibid.) is described in the most general terms.

Attempts have been made to explain these differences and omissions by differences in the sources of the compiler or editor or by the faultiness of his information as the result of his distance in time from the events or by political objectives and suchlike. These explanations of the critics have one thing in common, viz. the subjective aim of blurring over the *archaic and utopian* character of Josh. It is this blurring over which next claims our attention.

ALT'S CONJECTURES ABOUT THE LISTS OF BOUNDARIES
AND CITIES

In Josh 13-19 Alt found official "documents" of various date [7]. In the chapters on the distribution of the territory west of the Jordan he distinguishes a list of *boundaries* and two different lists of *cities*. The boundary list divides the whole western territory, from the River of Egypt to the Ladder of Tyre, entirely amongst seven tribes: Judah, Benjamin, Ephraim, Manasseh, Zebulun, Asher, Naphtali. It does not include Simeon, Dan and Issachar. It contains an ideal element, in that it apportions the *whole* Land, including even areas which had not been conquered. But the detailed and precise delineation of the inner (inter-tribal) boundaries proves that it is based on the actual distribution of the Land amongst the tribes. Alt thinks that this list was made in the pre-monarchic period. The ideal distribution of the *whole* Land gives expression to the tribes' demand for the acquisition of areas not yet conquered.

On to the list of boundaries have been grafted lists of cities which, in various respects, cannot be reconciled with it. These lists apportion the Land amongst all the Twelve Tribes, including Simeon, Dan and Issachar, though, in fact, the collator of the lists does not know either the cities of Simeon or the cities of Dan. He apportions the territories of these two tribes artificially, giving to Simeon the first district of the list of the cities of Judah (15 28-32; vide 19 1-7). About the boundaries of Dan he possessed no tradition and so he makes up the territory of Dan

---

7) In various papers: Landnahme, Judas Gaue, Stammesgrenzen, Ortsliste

from an area belonging to Judah and an area belonging to
Ephraim (vide infra). The purpose of all this is to complete the
number of twelve portions. In the city lists Alt singles out the
list of the cities of Judah (and Simeon), Benjamin and Dan as
a special unit. Its peculiar characteristic is that, unlike the other
lists, it divides (in the case of the territories of Judah and Benjamin) the cities into *districts*. It is on the basis of an examination of the northern boundary of this area that Alt fixes the
character and date of the list. It is a well-known fact, and one
which greatly exercises the critics' powers of explanation, that
the city list contains no mention of the cities of Ephraim and
Manasseh. Hence a space is left empty here. However, we find
that the territories of Benjamin and Dan encroach upon this
empty space. In 18 21-23 Jericho, Bethel and Ophrah are assigned
to Benjamin, though these cities in fact belonged to Ephraim
and were included in the northern kingdom (v. Josh 16 1-2
18 13 1 Ki 12 29 Am 7 10-13 et al. 1 Ki 16 34 2 Ki 2 4-5)[8]. The
cities of Dan reach to the outskirts of Jaffa (Josh 19 46).
Thus they occupy an area north of Gezer which is on the
southern boundary line of Ephraim (16 3). This leads us to the
conclusion that the list was drawn up at a time when the
Kingdom of Ephraim no longer existed and Judah was extending
its border northwards. In 2 Ki 23 15 it is related that Josiah
was active in Bethel, i. e. he annexed part of Ephraim to his
own kingdom. Alt goes further and conjectures that Josiah also
conquered, in unknown circumstances, the area north of Ekron
which in Joshua is considered part of the territory of Dan.
Accordingly, the lists of the cities of Judah, Benjamin and Dan
go back to a single official document, viz: the list of the cities
and districts of the *Kingdom of Judah at the time of Josiah.*
The editor cut up the original document, piecing together from
it the territories of the three tribes.

Alt distinguishes a special list of cities in Josh 21 10-39, in the

---

8) Ophrah is identified with Et-tayibe, north-east of Bethel, which is perhaps Ephron of 2 Chr 13 19.

description of the territory of the four Galilean tribes[9]. Here boundary delineations are mixed up with an enumeration of cities. Hence, apart from the ancient boundary list, the editor had in his hands a further source which included the cities of Galilee. Now how could a biblical author have come by the names of the cities of Galilee? This difficult problem is solved by Alt in characteristic fashion: he finds here a fresh official "document". The Assyrians made Galilee part of a district which they called "Megiddo". At the time of the collapse of the Assyrian Empire, the conquests of Josiah brought him to Megiddo. The Assyrian list of the cities of Galilee fell into the hands of Josiah's officials and from it the editor of Josh drew his information about the cities of the four Galilaean tribes. It is also possible that Josiah's officials themselves drew up a list of cities and that the editor received it from them. But it is obvious to Alt that, without an official "document", the editor could not have done his work.

Alt's views were accepted in principle by Noth, despite certain differences of opinion on individual points. In a series of detailed studies Noth reinforced and rounded off Alt's views. His conclusions are embodied in his Commentary to Josh. Noth belongs to that category of scholars who have carried to extremes the critico-literary analysis which serves them as a means of reconciling any text with their preconceived theories and of getting rid of the clearest evidence by excisions, erasures, and alterations. According to Noth, the Book of Joshua is the work of a collector (a "Sammler"), a recensionist (a "Bearbeiter"), and an editor, plus various expanders, all of whose topographical knowledge left much to be desired. They did not understand the documents in their possession; they even sometimes made mistakes such as would not be made by a schoolboy. Then came a "later hand" and added something, followed by another still "later hand" who inserted new matter into the text without any regard to the context. Only by such desperate measures is it possible to make Josh fit into the "theory" somehow. I fear that this does not argue well for the theory.

9) In his article "Ortsliste".

MOWINCKEL'S CRITICISM

The theories of Alt and Noth have been cleverly criticized by Mowinckel[10]. He rejects their literary analysis. He likewise rejects the search for "documents", the attempt to find in every nuance of the material a sign of the combination, association and abbreviation of "documents"; to find trace of a "document" even in two or three words. He rejects the assumption that the editor of Josh took everything from written sources. But on the factual side Mowinckel accepts several of Alt's and Noth's opinions. He agrees that the list of the cities of Judah, Simeon Benjamin and Dan is based upon the district list of Josiah's kingdom. He likewise accepts the view that the compiler of Josh did not know the boundaries of Dan, Simeon and Issachar, nor the boundaries of the Transjordanian tribes. The compiler possessed various traditions about the border between Ephraim and Manasseh and about Manasseh's northern border. He tried to find some way out of the confusion which enveloped all these questions (v. infra). Mowinckel rejects the view that the boundary list originated in the period of the Judges. The complete distribution of the Land amongst the tribes presupposes a juridico-religious doctrine, according to which the whole land of Canaan, from the River of Egypt to the Ladder of Tyre, was given to Israel by the word of God and therefore Israel has the right to inherit it in its entirety. Such a doctrine did not take shape before the time of David. Only a central political autho-

---

10) In his study "Josua 13-19".

The Portions of the Tribes

rity would have been interested in such a demand and in its juridico-religious sanction. The national programme expressed in the boundary list postulates the idea of "The Greater Land of Israel" and the real kingdom which aspired to the realization of this idea. This is not a tribal programme. The tribes conquered what they could, without any programme. Mowinckel agrees with the view, which Noth was particularly at pains to prove, that the tribes were organized in an amphictyonic union. But the amphictyony was religious and cultic, and not concerned with the wars of conquest. Moreover, it contained not twelve tribes, but only ten, as is allegedly proved by Ju 5. It did not include Judah and the other southern tribes. At that time Judah was entirely separate from "Israel".

For this reason we should not search in Josh 13-19 for actual "documents" from the period of the Conquest. Such documents never existed. There was no genuine historical tradition about the Conquest of the Land, not even in Ju 1. Ju 1, which belongs to J, merely summarizes and crystallizes the stage reached in the occupation of the Land in the time of David and Solomon. Josh 13-19 also contain such a summary — but of much later date. These chapters belong to P and are not the work of an "editor" who made a collection of "documents", but of an author and of an "intelligent author" at that, who drew on *a living tradition*, a tradition which was still preserved by the people of his time, the early days of the Second Temple. His idea is the politico-religious idea of a Land of Canaan given in its entirety to Israel; and it is this idea which conditions his descriptions of the division of the Land in the time of Joshua. For all that, he takes his factual information about the portions of the tribes from the tradition which was kept alive by the inhabitants of the Land in his time. For, seeing that in the time of the Second Temple the Jewish population still remembered its tribal affiliations, it was possible even then to construct a description of the tribal territories. The author also made use of Ju 1 and other Biblical sources. He made further additions of his own, with a view to filling the lacunae in the tradition and adapting it to his purpose. His description of the inter-tribal boundaries really is grounded in the actual situation which came into being in the period of the Judges, the tradition of which was preserved until his own time. The districts of Judah and Benjamin are defined by him according to the territorial division of Josiah's Kingdom which was likewise still known to his contemporaries. The boundaries of the Transjordanian tribes being unknown to him, he had to be content with listing their important cities. To the problem created by the lack of any tradition about the boundaries of Simeon and Dan he found the following solution. He knew from Ju 1 17 that the city of *Hormah* belonged to Simeon, so he accordingly assigns to that tribe Josiah's southern district in which Hormah lay. The case of Dan he treats similarly: the names of several cities which had formerly been inhabited by Dan were known to him from Biblical sources, and he accordingly assigns to Dan the Josianic district in which these cities were found, leaving the boundaries undefined. In the case of Issachar the boundaries were unknown to him, for the reason previously given by Alt—that Issachar was not an independent tribe. But he did know of various cities whose inhabitants traced back their descent to Issachar and these he listed, without fixing any boundaries. The cities of Ephraim and Manasseh are not listed by him, because their territory was in his day inhabited by the *Samaritans*. By this omission the author reveals his *Jewish* feelings (a view already expressed by Wellhausen[11]).

---

11) Composition des Hexateuchs, p. 133.

FLUCTUATIONS OF THE NORTHERN BORDER OF BENJAMIN

Of all these theories, that of Alt (accepted even by his opponents) — that the territory of Judah-Benjamin-Dan is identical with Josiah's kingdom — appears to rest on firm ground. If this theory is correct, it follows that the Book of Joshua was compiled certainly after the period of Josiah. However, the theory only appears sound: in fact it is groundless. It stands or falls on the argument that the territory of Benjamin-Dan in Josh encroaches upon that of Ephraim. And this argument is incapable of genuine proof.

There are three points at which the territory of Benjamin seemingly encroaches upon the boundary of Ephraim: Jericho, Bethel and Ophrah. But Jericho and Bethel are border-points (Josh 16 1-2 18 12-13). Ophrah is listed in 18 23 after Happarah and it may be that it is not Et-tayibeh (Ephron) in Ephraim at all, but another city in Benjamin. Still, even if we do identify it with Et-tayibeh, it is still very near to Bethel and should also be regarded as a city close to the border. Thus the apparent encroachment is no more than the shifting of a *border-strip*. Not a single Ephraimite city of the interior was included in Benjamin-Judah. This border fluctuation would require a special political explanation, if it were unique. But in fact such fluctuations are found in Josh *on almost every border*. It is a fact that in Josh the same communities are listed as border-points belonging equally to the tribes on either side of the border. We find such common points not only on the borders of Judah-Benjamin, but in other places too. Beth-shemesh, Timnah and Ekron are border-points of Judah (15 10-11), yet they are listed among the cities of Dan

(19 41-4). Hammichmethath is a border-point common to Ephraim and Manasseh (16 6 17 7). Heshbon is a border-point common to Reuben (13 17) and Gad (26); Mahanaim to Gad (ibid.) and half of Manasseh (30). Similarly, we find that, in the lists of cities, border cities (or those near the border) are listed in the territories of both the tribes on either side of the border. Beth-arabah and Kiriath-jearim are included amongst the cities of Judah (15 60-61 cf. esp. 18 14), whereas in 18 22 28 (according to the Septuagint text) the territory of Benjamin "encroaches" at these two points on that of Judah [12]. At Zorah, Eshthaol and Ekron (15 33 45) and Beth-shemesh (19 16) the territory of Judah "encroaches" upon that of Dan (19 41-42), or vice versa. At Jerusalem, Judah (according to 16 63) encroaches upon Benjamin (18 28). Haddaberath is included in both Zebulun (19 12) and Issachar (21 28). Beth-shemesh is listed in both Issachar (19 22) and Naphtali (ibid. 38) [13].

In view of all this, the shifting of the border Jericho-Bethel is not to be regarded as a special phenomenon, nor does it imply any political conquest. On the contrary, the above facts show that the boundary-lines in Josh have no *political* or *administrative* significance whatsoever. Political and administrative boundaries must be clear and unambiguous, which the boundaries of Josh are not. The purpose of the delineation of the tribal territories given in this book is purely *historical*. Josh records the distribution of the Land amongst the tribes and describes ethnographic groups (both real and ideal) in general terms, without any intention of drawing exact lines. Such a description *belongs to an earlier date* than any political and administrative division. It is a description

12) Alt, Judas Gaue, p. 105, discusses these fluctuations which, in his view, are to be explained by the cutting up of the original documents and the inserting of the fragments in different places. This is not an explanation. But even if it were, it can surely just as well explain the fluctuation of the line Jericho-Bethel.

13) Bethel and Ai (Aija) are listed in Ezr 2 28; Neh 11 31 amongst the cities of Benjamin, whereas according to 1 Chr 7 28 they belong to Ephraim.

which includes in the tribal territories even places which, in the author's day, were politically independent: Gezer, the cities of the Emeq, the cities of the Shephelah, etc. The political association of Jericho and Bethel with the Northern *Kingdom* proves nothing at all about their ethnographic associations in the author's day. Moreover, the fact that he lists the same border communities in the territories of both bordering tribes surely shows that in the border-strips there were also mixed communities. In the territory of Tappuach, where this mixture was particularly marked, the author specifically mentions it (16 8-9   17 8-9 ; cf. infra). It might be better if scholars, instead of indicting the editors of Josh for muddle-headedness and unintelligent and slipshod cutting up of "documents", were to free themselves of their own fundamental confusion of ethnographic with political and administrative boundaries [14].

14) On this question v. the sound argumentation of Simons in his study, Structure, p. 203, note 2. Only Simons stresses the difference between "the tribal boundaries" and "terms of modern state-frontiers". But this is not something that applies only to modern frontiers. Undoubtedly it was just as impossible in the Ancient East for *inhabited localities* to be claimed by two states or districts without this giving rise to daily friction. The tribal borders are *in no sense* political or administrative boundaries; neither in ancient nor in modern usage.

THE BOUNDARIES OF DANITE TERRITORY

Entirely imaginary is the assertion that Dan encroaches on Ephraim.

This assertion owes its existence to Alt's astonishing error in his understanding of the boundary list in Josh. Alt holds that the boundary list *did not leave any free space for Dan between Judah and Ephraim*. Since Alt himself insists that, according to the boundary list, the tribal territories formed a continuous, unbroken sequence, it follows, in his opinion, that the list supposes the territories of Judah and Ephraim to be immediately contiguous to each other: in other words, that these tribes *posses a common boundary*. Indeed, Alt says that the coastal strip was divided amongst Judah, Ephraim, Manasseh and Asher[15]. This strange error leads him to the conclusion that Dan had no territory with fixed boundaries and that the portion of Dan as described in Josh 19 40-46 is in the area which the boundary list assigns *partly to Judah and partly to Ephraim*[16]. This composite area is not an ancient tribal unit, but the district "Ekron" of Josiah's kingdom[17].

Unfortunately, the premiss of all this theory is completely mistaken. It is *not* the case that, according to the boundary list, Judah and Ephraim have a common border. The northern boundary of Judah runs as follows: the Jordan-Beth-hoglah etc., — Kiriath-jearim etc., — Ekron-Javneel — the sea (15 5-12). The southern border of Ephraim is: the Jordan-Jericho etc., — Beth

---

15) Stammesgrenzen, p. 16, and ibid. note 2.
16) Ortsliste, p. 66.   17) Judas Gaue, p. 115.

Horon — Gezer — the sea (16 1-3). Judah and Ephraim are thus separated by *a vacant strip* from *the Jordan to the sea*. Even in the coastal strip there *is* a space between Judah and Ephraim. According to Josh 18 11-15, Benjamin received the eastern half of the unoccupied area, up to the line Beth-horon — Kiriath-jearim. The western half remained vacant. Hence the boundary list allows for *an unoccupied portion from the* line Beth-horon — Kiriath-jearim to the sea. We know from Ju that the tribe of Dan tried to establish itself in this portion. Josh 19 40-48 actually assigns this territory to Dan. The area in question lies between Judah and Ephraim and has its *own special* boundaries, even according to the boundary list.

Alt and his followers were misled by the fact that in Josh 19 40-46 the boundaries of Dan are not explicitly described. They argue that the compiler left out the boundaries of Dan because he did not know them, not having found any such boundaries in his sources. But, if he really did leave them out (and that is still doubtful, v. note 18) the reason was certainly just that the boundaries of Dan had been *absolutely and completely fixed* by those of its three neighbours: Judah, Benjamin, Ephraim. Indeed, Dan is *unique* in that its boundaries were completely fixed by those of its neighbours. The boundaries were not explicitly described, but they are implicitly included in the boundary list. Fixing the boundaries of Benjamin automatically fixes those of Dan: on the east — Beth-horon, Kiriath-jearim (the border of Benjamin); on the south — Kiriath-jearim, Mount Seir, Kesalon, Beth-shemesh, Timnah, Ekron, Javneel, the sea (border of Judah); on the north — Beth-horon, Gezer, the sea (border of Ephraim). There is some vagueness about the line Gezer — the sea, but this is simply because the border of Ephraim is itself vague. Moreover, the description of Dan's territory enables us to complete the delineation of Ephraim's boundary and assume that its "sea" point is "over against Jaffa" (19 46). The line curved north-wards: from Gezer to "over against Jaffa". The later ethnographic and political fate of this area does not concern us at all here. For us the important fact is that, on the line Beth-horon — Gezer, the territory of Dan, as described in Josh 19, does not encroach on the territory of Ephraim.

The list of Danite cities does not even include Beth-horon and Gezer themselves; and the same is true of the line Gezer — the sea. Nor is there amongst the cities of Dan a single one south of the border of Judah. The territory assigned to Dan lies entirely *between* the boundaries of Judah and Ephraim [18].

Noth does not accept Alt's false premiss, but he does accept and attempt to find support for the conclusion which Alt deduces from it. Noth argues (Comm. on Josh, p. 81) that, according to the ancient boundary list, all the vacant area between Judah and Ephraim belonged to Benjamin and that the line from Beth-horon to Kiriath-jearim was drawn by the recensionist himself, in order to leave space for Dan. This is simply a figment of Noth's imagination which has no support in the text. The list of the cities of Benjamin (Josh 18 21-28) does not contain a single city west of Kiriath-jearim. According to Ju 1 34-35 13 2 25 et al., it was in this corner (west of Kiriath-jearim) that Dan fought for its territorial portion. Ju 1 assigns to Dan, as to the rest of the tribes, a portion by lot, and Dan fights for the actual possession of the allotted territory, but is not successful. However, even if we accept Noth's fiction, it does not in fact make any difference to the matter under discussion. For obviously, even according to this fiction, the ancient boundary list would still leave a *space* between Judah and Ephraim. The "recensionist's" innovation would consist merely of dividing the area into two and giving the western half to Dan. But we know that *the boundaries of this section* (from the line Beth-horon—Kiriath-jearim to the sea)

---

18) But in fact the argument that the author is not describing boundaries at all in Josh 19 41-46 also requires further study. True, there is no boundary-drawing in the usual style of the Book of Joshua. But it is very possible that the list includes a specification of "border-points" (Grenzfixpunkte in Noth's sense), without any connecting words. Ir-shemesh, Timnah and Ekron are border-points of Judah. Gibbethon is apparently a point on the border between Ephraim and the Philistines (v. 1 Ki 15 27 16 15). In v. 46, where "the border over against Jaffa" is mentioned, the border of Ephraim on the line Gezer—the sea may be meant. It is very possible that in vv. 44-46 all the border-points of this line are listed.

were fixed by the ancient boundary list. This would mean that the "recensionist" did not take parts of Judah and Ephraim to make up a portion for Dan, but gave him a continuous and vacant area (according to Noth's fanciful invention—from the territory of Benjamin). The *boundaries* of this area, the eastern end of which he himself fixed, were of course absolutely clear in his mind. Thus, in any case, the territory of Dan has fixed boundaries in the "recensionist's" boundary list (which in turn is based on the ancient list), and it has no connection with any Josianic district.

On the other hand, it is obvious what the author *does not really know*: Dan's *northern* portion! He knows as much as that Dan migrated northwards (19 47). But the chorographers of that time had not yet "drawn the map" of its territory. If the author had been a late scribe, and if he had merely wanted to make up the full number of twelve portions, what was to prevent him from including the *real* portion of Dan in the north? He could have recounted that Dan's lot fell out between Judah and Ephraim, but that when its border passed out of its control it obtained a portion in the north; with the usual continuation: "And the border of his inheritance" etc. He could even have related that it was Joshua himself who advised Dan to migrate to the north (in the manner of the stories in 14 6-15 and 17 14-18) and assigned them a new inheritance *for the future*. The fact that the author describes *only* the *unreal* portion of Dan proves that he lived *before* the period of "from Dan unto Beersheba". He does not conceive of the land which was divided amongst the tribes of Israel as containing the northern territory of Dan. (V. infra).

JOSH CONTAINS NO REFERENCE TO JOSIAH'S KINGDOM

The truth is that the view, that the territory of Judah-Benjamin-Dan is identical with Josiah's enlarged kingdom, is at no point consonant with the sources and can be maintained only by imaginative conjectures and by a systematic "revision" of the text based solely on dogmatic assumptions.

In 2 Ki 23 15-18 we are told that Josiah extended his work of cultic purification to the area of Bethel. But later in the same passage (19-20) it is related that, at the very same time, he also took action "in the cities of Samaria". Hence, if we are to conclude from this that he added northern areas to Judah, we shall also have to include the cities of Samaria within his kingdom. How then is it possible to assume that the slight displacement of the border in Josh 17 21-22 in the strip of territory from Jericho to Bethel indicates an enlargement of Josiah's kingdom? Why are the other cities which he annexed not listed? Why is not a single Ephraimite city of the interior mentioned?

In actual fact, 2 Ki 23 contains no reference to annexation and territorial expansion. The collapse of Assyrian power presented Josiah with the opportunity of undertaking certain cultic activities in the cities of the north, undoubtedly with the consent of the remnants of the Israelite population. He therefore set to work in *the cities* of Samaria, but not in Samaria itself. The attempts made to portray Josiah as a military hero bent on restoring the Kingdom of David are devoid of authority: the Book of Kings cannot recount *even one successful war* fought by this righteous and tragic king. Hence Alt's conjecture, that Josiah conquered the area round Ekron (territory of Dan), must

37

be regarded as a product of the imagination pure and simple. At various times Benjamite and Judahite communities established themselves in the territory of Dan : Ayalon, Timnah (1 Chr 8 13 2 Chr 11 10 28 18), Lod, Hadid, Ono (1 Chr 8 12 Neh 11 34-35 ; et al.). But the majority of the region remained Philistine. The portion of Dan as drawn in Josh is *unreal*.

Both the portion of Dan (Josh 19 40-46) and the western border of Judah, viz: the fifth district in Judah's list of cities, comprising Ekron, Ashdod and Gaza (15 45-47), point to one and the same fact: that the list of cities is *not* a real official list and that it has nothing to do with the kingdom of Josiah. So far from there being any ground for the identification of Dan's portion with the fifth district of Judah, it actually involves doing serious violence to a perfectly clear and intelligible text. The territory of Dan and the fifth district have a common border-point in Ekron — a regular occurrence in these chapters, as has already been observed — but they are two entirely different areas. In Josh 15 45 (territory of Judah) Ekron is the *northern* border-point of an area stretching from Ekron to the Wadi of Egypt, whereas in 19 43 (territory of Dan) it is a *southern* border-point of a region stretching from Ekron to "over against Jaffa". Noth (Josua, p. 69) maintains that the recensionist left Ekron (in 15 45) as a clue-word, after transferring the list of cities to 19 40-46, and in this way became involved in self-contradiction. In Noth's opinion, 15 46 was added by "a later hand" and 47 by "someone" still later. By such tampering with the text does Noth convert two areas, the one Judahite and the other Danite, into a single area. In addition to this he further "corrects" the western boundary which had caused some embarrassment to Alt: with the help of two "later hands" he expunges the whole area from Ekron to the Wadi of Egypt which was not included in the Kingdom of Josiah. But what ground is there for all these doings? What right have we to attribute to the recensionist the leaving of clue-words and then accuse him of self-contradiction? And what right have we to convert two areas into one, simply to preserve Alt's theory? True, the list of western boundary cities is unreal. But in this respect the city list is like the boundary list: all this area from

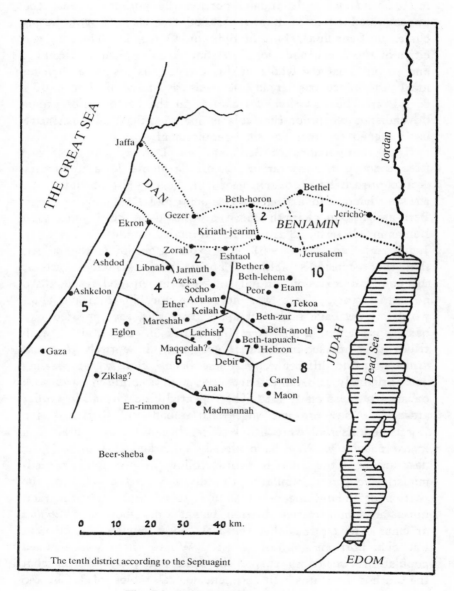

THE GREAT SEA

Jaffa

DAN

Bethel

Beth-horon

Gezer

Ekron

2

1

Jericho

Kiriath-jearim

BENJAMIN

Jerusalem

Jordan

Zorah

Ashdod

Libnah

2

Eshtaol

Bether

10

Jarmuth

Azeka

Socho

Beth-lehem

Etam

Ashkelon

4

Ether

Adulam

Peor

Tekoa

5

Keilah

Mareshah

Beth-zur

Eglon

Lachish

3

Beth-anoth

9

Gaza

Maqqedah?

Beth-tapuach

6

7

Hebron

JUDAH

Ziklag?

Debir

8

Dead Sea

Carmel

Anab

Maon

En-rimmon

Madmannah

Beer-sheba

| 0 | 10 | 20 | 30 | 40 | km. |

The tenth district according to the Septuagint

EDOM

The Districts of Judah and Benjamin

the Wadi of Egypt to Ekron and from Ekron to Jaffa *is contained in the boundary list*. In Judah's portion the author includes the unconquered cities of Ekron, Ashdod and Gaza, just as he includes in Benjamin Jebus, in Ephraim Gezer, in Manasseh the cities of the Emeq and Dor, in Asher Acco, Apheq and Rehov, and so on. That the whole of this territory is no more than an ideal inheritance has already been clearly stated by him in 13 2 sqq. 19 47. The inclusion of this area in the list of cities provides indisputable proof that this is not an official administrative list designed to meet practical requirements.

That the portions of Benjamin and Dan were not cut out from a single administrative list of the whole Josianic country is also proved by the duplications in the city list of Judah, on the one hand, and in that of Benjamin and Dan, on the other. Beth-arabah and Kiriath-jearim are listed in both Judah and Benjamin (15 60-61 18 22-28); Zorah and Eshtaol are listed in Judah and Dan (15 33 19 41). The explanations of Noth and Alt that the recensionist left overlapping names as clue-words at the points of excision, or did his work in slipshod fashion, are not satisfactory. There was no reason for him to leave clue-words, as we have said. But apart from this, the repeated city names appear in a different framework in the case of each tribe: they are set in different groupings, in entirely *different districts*, and in different city enumerations. Here we are dealing with originally *separate* districts, not with a confused patchwork collated by careless scribes. The repeated cities are all in border areas. We may presume that Beth-arabah and Kiriath-jearim, Zorah and Eshtaol were listed twice, because they contained a *mixed population*. We have already remarked that in Josh the description of the tribal territories follows ethnographic, not administrative, lines. Similarly, the division into *districts* of the portion of Judah-Simeon-Benjamin is to be understood, in fact, not as an administrative division, but as a distribution to *families* or clans. The truth is that these are not administrative *districts*, but clan portions (v. Josh 17 5 14). Where there was a mixed population two tribes shared the same strip; and this is what the author indicates. (In the genealogical tables of 1 Chr 2-8 the cities themselves have already become the names of heads of families). For this reason the city lists of Judah, Simeon, Benjamin and Dan are originally separate descriptions of the inheritances of *tribes* and *families* and were not cut out by a "recensionist" from a single document.

The author mentions, in the portion of Dan, only Zorah and Eshtaol (and in 21 16 also Beth-shemesh), but amongst the cities of Judah and Benjamin he does not mention Ayalon, Timnah, Lod, Hadid and Ono. This fact fixes his date as *before* the establishment of these Judahite communities in the portion of Dan. Only Zorah and Eshtaol, and perhaps Beth-shemesh, were real Danite settlements in this area. We may suppose that, with the northern migration of Dan, Zorah, Eshtaol and Beth-shemesh were annexed to Judah. This is the stage reflected in our text: Zorah and Ehstaol belong to Judah, while the rest of the territory is Amorite-Philistine. This is in keeping with the author's ignorance of the northern portion of Dan. His picture reflects the situation created by the movement of Dan northwards, at the very moment of the migration.

THE PORTION OF SIMEON

Only in the light of the above explanation is it possible to understand the description of Simeon's portion (19 1-9).

Most superficial is the view that the author, having no information about Simeon's portion, drew it by conjecture from Ju 1 17, more or less as in the case of Dan: he gave Simeon that section of the first Josianic district of Judah in which Hormah was listed (Josh 15 30). The view of Alt and his followers, that the author adopted *the same procedure* for both Dan and Simeon [19], originates in Alt's mistaken opinion that the portion of Dan, as given in Josh 19 40-46, is partly in Judah and partly in Ephraim. However, since Dan really has boundaries of its own, as we have seen, there is no conceivable similarity between Dan and Simeon. The portion of Dan has *its own proper* boundaries, but it is unreal. Whereas the portion of Simeon has *no* boundaries of its own, but is real. It is the only portion *of which all the cities* are listed within the territory of another tribe (Judah). Only of Simeon is it explicitly said (19 9) that it obtained its inheritance in another tribe. The author of Josh does not base his delineation of the tribal territories on literary evidence or on conjecture arising from confusion, ignorance and an attempt to smooth over difficulties. He describes real facts which he knows at first hand. Nor is it correct that he "mechanically" copies out a section of Judah's first district and assigns it to Simeon. In actual fact, he assigns to Simeon *two* territorial areas: one in

19) v. Alt, Ortliste, p. 66; Mowinckel, Josua 13-19, p. 27-28.

the first district (15 26-32) and the other in the fourth (ibid. 42). The latter is in the Shephelah and has no connection with Hormah in the Negev. Moreover, the two strips appear in special associations and special city enumerations, quite distinct from those of Judah. Even Noth (Josua, p. 85) is at a loss to harmonize all this with the theory, though here too he conjures up the shade of the "later hand". The author of Josh portrays a situation which had come into being at the beginning of the period of the Judges. In Ju 1₃ 17 Simeon has a "lot" of its own which Judah helps it to conquer. But the special military alliance between Judah and Simeon brings about the absorption of Simeon's portion into Judah's, so that in Saul's time the cities of Simeon, including Hormah, are already part of Judah (1 Sam 30 26-30). The Simeonite communities are mixed and their "lot" has merged with the "lot" of Judah, without their tribal unity being thereby dissolved. They were settled in two areas and organized in two clans. These areas, though in Judah, are not co-terminous with the Judahite areas, but constitute special ethnographic units. At a later date the Simeonites expand southwards and conquer new areas (1 Chr 4 34-47), but this expansion is not mentioned by the author of Josh. He knows only the situation which came into being in the time of the Judges and he knows it accurately and at first hand, not from literary research and by conjecture. What he describes has nothing at all to do with any administrative division of Josiah's kingdom.

Did the author of Josh know the boundaries of Simeon's special "lot" which is mentioned in Ju 1₃ ? It may well be that he did not. The process of Simeon's territorial absorption took place early and was quickly over, so that someone living at the beginning of the period of the Judges may already have been unable to determine such boundaries. Dan fought for its inheritance until the period of the Philistine wars, whereas only a short time was required for Simeon's assimilation. On the other hand, it is possible that he did know the boundaries, but did not think it necessary to specify them. For, to a certain extent, Simeon remained within the confines of its old "lot" and inherited a real portion there. It is this real portion which the author wanted to describe.

JEBUS

Thus we find that the view, that the list of the cities of Judah-Simeon, Benjamin and Dan was drawn from the district list of Josiah's kingdom, has no support whatever in the plain rendering of the Biblical text.

The place occupied by *Jerusalem* in this list (and throughout Josh) suffices to rule out such a view. Is it really possible that, in an official district list of the seventh century, Jerusalem — the capital of a great king, the glorious city of God — would have been mentioned in the terms used here? In the city list, as in the boundary list, Jerusalem is still *Jebus!* This name is followed by the explanation: "that is Jerusalem" (18 28). It is listed at the end of Benjamin's second district — a remote place, one of the twenty six cities of Benjamin. To the list of Judah's cities is attached the note, that Jerusalem was still occupied by the Jebusite (15 63). This is in keeping with the fact that *Hebron* is here called *Kiriath-arbah* (15 54), and *Kiriath-jearim Kiriath-baal* (60). Noth, of course, expunges even these unmistakable signs — all for the sake of the theory.

The fact that the Book of Joshua, while unable to describe Dan's real historical portion, assigns to that tribe a territory which was never occupied by it, is the clearest possible evidence of the archaic and utopian character of the land distribution list of the tribes. It is not the case that the ancient tribal inheritance took shape only as a result of the actual war of conquest, and that the tribes identified what they had actually managed to conquer with what they had been given by the

Lord [20]. Such an interpretation does not fit the facts. According to Ju 1 the tribes considered even cities which they had not conquered as part of their territory. The tribal portion is an a priori postulate, not a post-conquest rationalization. The boundary list follows a firm, clear-cut design, quite independent of later history. Thus Ephraim never conquered *Gezer*, nor did it ever settle there: this city was given to Solomon by Pharaoh (1 Ki 9 16), just as *Ziklag* was given to David by Achish (1 Sam 27 6). For all that, Gezer remained in the lists a city of Ephraim. The Benjamites never conquered *Jerusalem*, nor did they ever enjoy sole occupation of it: it was conquered by David, the Judahite, and after its conquest became the royal city, belonging to no tribe. For all that, Jerusalem remained in the lists a city of Benjamin. Examples could be multiplied, but we shall take only the special case of Dan. Dan managed to obtain a firm hold only on the edge of its portion. The portion assigned to it in Josh is not the sum total of what it conquered: it is a utopian inheritance. Dan's history is bound up with its northern territory, whereas the Danite portion given in the inheritance list precedes the tribe's history. The same is true of all the other portions. The list of inheritances does not sum up an ethnographic situation which came into being as the result of separate tribal wars. Rather, the distribution of the Land took shape right at the beginning of the tribes' history, in the very period of the Conquest. It was an act of *national* policy, an agreed covenant between *all* the tribes of Israel, a covenant of the tribes which *conquered the Land*. All the attempts to find tribes which were not included in the ancient boundary list arise from the preconceived notion that the union of the tribes of Israel is only a late accomplishment. This prejudice is refuted by the utopian character of the boundary list. (V. infra, pp. 47 sqq.).

20) Mowinckel, Josua 13-19, p. 16-17.

THE GALILEAN TRIBES

The description of the territories of the Galilean tribes is fragmentary and incomplete. It contains a confused mixture of boundary lines and city lists. In the territory of Issachar, in particular, we find only a small relic of a boundary line (19 22). But this cannot support the assumption of Alt and Mowinckel that Issachar had no fixed boundaries or that the author did not know of the tribe's boundaries [21]. It is no argument at all to maintain that Issachar was not always autonomous, but subject to the Canaanites and obliged to seek the support of other tribes, and that for this reason its boundaries were not fixed. The tribal portion, actually and ideally, is an *ethnic*, not a political, entity. Included in the tribes' ideal inheritance are even Canaanite and Philistine regions which were politically independent. Moreover, the actual assumption that Issachar was not autonomous goes too far. Gen 49 15 is weak and inconclusive evidence. In Ju 5 16 Issachar is a martial tribe, like the others. If Dan, which never occupied its portion, nonetheless has fixed boundaries, is there any reason for denying the same to Issachar? Even supposing that Issachar was not "autonomous", it still occupied its own territory and must in any case have had some boundaries [22]. Assumptions such as those above cannot be based

21) v. Alt, Stammesgrenzen, pp. 13-14, 18-19; Ortsliste, 64-68; Mowinckel, Josua 13-19, pp. 28-30.

22) Mowinckel's view is most astonishing. In his opinion, the author lived at the beginning of the Second Temple and drew his information from an

on our fragmentary text. That Issachar did have fixed boundaries is proved by the fact that the north-eastern border of *Manasseh* is described in Josh 17 10 as the border of *Asher and Issachar* [23]. If the author does not give details of this border of Manasseh, the reason is to be found in his assumption that the border of Asher and Issachar is fixed and well-known. It makes no difference whether the author himself described it in his book and the description was then omitted from the extant text, or whether, for some reason or other, he did not describe it at all. A fixed boundary is also indicated by 17 11, where it is said that the district Beth-shean-Dor belonged "to Manasseh in Issachar and in Asher". Interpret this sentence as we may — even according to the (mistaken) interpretation of Alt and Mowinckel — the text clearly assumes that Issachar's portion is a well-defined, fixed entity. (V. infra, pp. 36 sqq.).

ethnographic tradition kept alive by the people. The local inhabitants still knew that they were descendants of Issachar. But of what importance to such a tradition is the fact that hundreds of years previously, before the Kingdom was ever founded, Issachar was not "autonomous"? If it was possible to fix the site of Issachar's settlement by the living tradition, why was is not possible to fix its boundaries? In the question of Issachar Mowinckel follows Alt. But Alt speaks of a gap in an *ancient* boundary-list dating back to the time of the Judges. There is thus some logic to his argument. But where is the logic in Mowinckel's case?

23) In 17 10 the text makes the border of *Manasseh* dependent on Issachar, and not the converse as Alt, Ortsliste, p. 67, maintains (in contradiction of his own words, ibid. p. 65). Here it is assumed that the border of Issachar is fixed and known. — This would also appear to be the intention in 17 7. "From Asher to Hammichmethath" means: from the northern border line formed by Asher-Issachar to the line of Hammichmethath, which has been described in 16 6. "Asher" is an abbreviation for "Asher and Issachar".

THE TRANSJORDANIAN TRIBES

The description of the portions of the Transjordanian tribes
(13 15-32) bears a stamp of its own. This description has come
down to us in its entirety, with none of the fragmentariness of
c. 19. In spite of this it contains no detail about boundaries.
Mowinckel rightly rejects Noth's attempt to find "documents"
here too (one comprising border points and a second comprising
a list of cities), together with a "recensionist" etc. [24] But Mowinckel himself is mistaken in thinking that the author was
ignorant of the borders of the Transjordanian tribes. If the author
could draw upon the living ethnological tradition for information
about "the important cities of those regions", why could he not
have used the same tradition to fix the boundaries? It is no
explanation to argue, as Mowinckel does, that Reuben had very
early ceased to be a distinct tribe. For he says himself that oral
tradition kept alive the record of the tribal differentiation. The
truth is that Josh contains no reference to the later fate of
Reuben; indeed, it is Reuben's portion which receives the most
detailed description. Moreover, the description of Transjordania
does contain a *clear*, if not *detailed*, *demarkation* of the boundaries of all the tribes. The author's description is not schematic,
nor is he concerned to satisfy the demands of modern pedantry.
But there is no indication that he did not have a clear picture
of the division of Transjordania amongst the tribes. Being an

---

24) Noth, ZDPV 1935, pp. 232 sqq; Comm. on Josh, pp. 50 sqq; Mowinckel, Josua 13-19, pp. 27, 32.

ancient scribe, he employs methods of description which were clear enough to his contemporaries.

To understand the special nature of the description of Transjordania, we must bear in mind the difference between the division of Transjordania and that of Canaan. In Canaan there were seven peoples and tens of city-states. The tribal portions did not fit the boundaries of either peoples or city-states. Hence the boundary lines of the tribes are entirely new and entirely artificial, having neither geographical (natural), nor historical (ethno-political), foundation. Such boundaries could be drawn only by means of a detailed demarkation of settlements or local topographical divisions. This was not the case in Transjordania. Here there were geo-historical units which the tribal boundaries fitted. Here there were three large territorial blocs: the kingdom of Og, king of Bashan; the old Amorite kingdom of Sihon (from the Jabbok to Heshbon); and the later Amorite-Moabite kingdom of Sihon (from Heshbon to the Arnon), vide Nu 21 24-35 Josh 12 1-5 13 9-13. There were also other blocs of territory: Bashan, Argov, Sixty Cities, Geshur, Maachath, Gilead, the cities of Gilead. All these were perspicuous expressions to the geographers of Conquest times; and it is against this background that Josh 13 describes the portions. "From Aroer which is on the bank of the river Arnon" (13 16) does not define a "point", but marks a complete *line* — a well-known historical, political and topographical boundary; namely, the *whole* southern border of the Moabite kingdom of Sihon, viz. the southern boundary of Reuben. "Heshbon" likewise (17) is not a "point", but a complete politico-historical boundary: the southern border of Sihon's old kingdom, viz. the northern boundary of Reuben. The ancient scribe, writing in terms of his times, could not have foreseen that Noth and Mowinckel would be here short of "points". Where the border of Gad curves or runs diagonally, he marks it in detail: from Heshbon to Ramath-hammizpeh, thence to Betonim, Mahanaim, and on to Debir (Lo-debar) and the edge of the Sea of Kinnereth (26-27). "From Mahanaim" in v. 30 marks the whole common border of Gad-Manasseh. From here onwards the scribe lists, in the portion of Manasseh, well-known territorial blocs: Bashan, Havoth-jair, half Gilead. It certainly never occurred to him that Noth would conclude from this that the "recensionist" knew of only *one* city of Manasseh — Mahanaim (Comm. on Josh, p. 55). Even the mention of *Ashtaroth* and *Edrei* (31) could not deliver the "recensionist" from this harsh judgment.

THE BOUNDARIES OF EPHRAIM AND MANASSEH

The boundary demarkation of *Ephraim and Manasseh* in Josh 16-17 constitutes an especially difficult literary and historical problem.

First of all, there is the remarkable fact that these chapters contain no list of the *cities* of Ephraim and Manasseh. Alt's political explanation, that this lacuna reflects the destruction of the Northern Kingdom and the extension of the Kingdom of Judah in Josiah's time, has already been dismissed as imaginary. It is inconceivable that the author would have described the extension of Josiah's kingdom in such a negative way: by *not* listing the cities which Josiah is assumed to have annexed to his kingdom. In fact, the whole Book of Joshua does not once mention the Destruction, nor even the *Kingdom itself;* and the "allusions" are merely figments of the imagination. Similarly, it cannot be supposed that the absence of a city list indicates an unfavourable attitude on the part of the author or editor to non-Jewish "Samaria" of the Second Temple. Hostility to "Samaria" found expression in segregation from the *Samaritans*, "the foes of Judah and Benjamin", and in fighting against them, not in giving up all claim to the *land* of Samaria and *its cities*. If our text contained the most detailed list of cities, it would doubtless be just as possible to interpret that as a hostile "allusion" to "Samaria"[25]. An explanation for the absence of the city list

25) Mowinckel, Josua 13-19, p. 33, does indeed find such an "allusion" in the list of the clans of Manasseh in Josh 17 2⁻6 : in giving these details about

can be found only in the history of the *Book* of Joshua. The lacuna is not to be charged to an *intentional act* on the part of the *author*, still less to his *ignorance*, seeing that he draws *the boundaries* in detail. He is both *concerned* and *competent* to describe the nature of the intricate border between Ephraim and Manasseh (16 9 17 7-9). He also specifies the Canaanite cities on the northern border of Manasseh. Hence, the absence of the city list can only be the result of its excision from one of *the later editions* of the ancient Book of Joshua. The scars left by that excision can still be recognized.

Chapters 16-17 present, structurally and textually, a most difficult problem which has greatly taxed the critics' powers.

According to the title (16 1), "the sons of Joseph" received a common lot. The title is followed by a description of the southern border of the *whole* portion of Joseph (1-3). However, vv. 5-6, instead of continuing with a description of the northern border of the whole portion, describe the southern and northern borders of the territory of *Ephraim*. In our text this description consists of an absurd confusion of boundary lines, as will be shown subsequently. V. 9 mentions "the cities set aside (הערים המבדלות) for the children of Ephraim in the inheritance of Manasseh", without any explanation of the meaning. Then in 17 1-11 comes a

---

the clans the author's intention is to stress that it is these clans to whom the Land belongs, and not the Samaritan rabble. But the question then arises: why did he not follow up this "allusion" with yet another "allusion" — the list of Manasseh's *cities*? Of course, 17 2-6 contains no "allusion". From the storyteller's point of view all the clans of Manasseh are the children of Gilead, the son of Machir, the son of Manasseh, as explained in Nu 26 28-34, cf. esp. Josh 17 3 (the genealogy of Zelophehad). In other words, some clans of Manasseh who received a "lot" at this juncture had already obtained their portion in Transjordania. Hence the author explains that the "lot" was given to "the rest" of Manasseh's sons. He gives a list of the clans only in the case of Manasseh, because that tribe alone had split into two. What he further particularly wants to explain is why the six sons of Gilead obtained *ten* portions (5-6). Thus the listing of the clans is demanded at this point by the story and is wholly devoid of "allusions".

description of the territory of *Manasseh*. 17 7-10 follows the intricacies of the inner boundary between Ephraim and Manasseh. Only the western half of the boundary, from Hammichmethath to the sea, is described. Vv. 8-10 return to the cities of Ephraim within the border of Manasseh. No details are given of the northern border of Manasseh or that of the territory of Joseph as a whole: we are merely told that it impinges upon Asher and Issachar (v. 10; in v. 7 this border is briefly indicated as: Asher). V. 11 describes the Canaanite region on the northern border of Manasseh.

Elliger expressed the view that a later editor changed the verse order in 16-17, placing *Ephraim* befor *Manasseh* [26]. In 16 4 Manasseh is mentioned before Ephraim, and in 17 1 it is emphasised that Manasseh is the first-born. In the original order of the verses, the description of Manasseh's border preceded that of Ephraim. Thus the correct sequence would be: 16 1-3 17 1-13 16 5-10. This view is accepted by *Noth* (Comm. to Josh, p. 72 sqq.) [27]. Noth is of the opinion that the ancient list of border-points used by the "recensionist" contained a description of a *single* portion—the portion of *Joseph* which bore the name of *Machir*. For in 17 1 it is stressed that the lot belonged "to the tribe of Manasseh, for he is the first-born of Joseph", that is to say: "to Machir, the first-born of Manasseh". By the *law of primogeniture* the whole inheritance belongs to Manasseh, the first-born of Joseph, and to Machir the first-born of Manasseh. In this inheritance of Machir a certain area was allotted to Ephraim; and it is this area which, in 16 9, is called "the cities set apart for the children of Ephraim in the inheritance of the children of Manasseh", and these are the cities mentioned also in 17 9. From Ju 5 14 we know that the portion of Manasseh formerly bore the name of Machir. And by this name it was called in the list of border-points too. The implication of the remarks about Machir in Josh 17 1-2 is: *de jure* all the inheritance belonged to Machir, but, seeing that Machir went off to Gilead,

---

26) Elliger, ZDPV 1930, pp. 265-309, cf. p. 267. On pp. 306-307 he combines 16 and 17.

27) V. also Noth, ZDPV 1935, pp. 201 sqq.

the inheritance was given *de facto* "to the remaining children of Manasseh".

This view is convincingly refuted by Simons[28], who shows that Noth's interpretation rests upon unsound subtleties of translation. But Simons does not go far enough and there is more to be added to his arguments. Noth translates והערים המבדלות (16 9): Die abgeteilten Städte, as if there were here no copulative waw indicating that these cities were an *addition* to the portion of Ephraim described in vv. 5-8. Most important of all, the alleged "law of primogeniture" by which the whole portion of Joseph belonged to Manasseh-Machir, is entirely imaginary. There never existed in Israel such a "law of primogeniture". From Deut 21 17 we learn that by the "law of primogeniture" the first-born inherited *a double share*. But a privilege of *majorat* did not exist in Israel even in the common inheritance law, still less in the matter of the distribution of the Land, which was not an *inheritance* but an allocation of territory amongst *conquerors*. The author's sole purpose in mentioning Machir and Gilead and their genealogy at this point is his wish to provide a reason for the duality of Manasseh's portion, and also to explain why the *six* children of Gilead the son of Machir received *ten* shares[29]. Furthermore, it is not to be supposed that the author would indicate the whole large area of Ephraim by such a phrase as "the cities set apart". These are simply the cities

---

28) Simons, Structure, pp. 191 sqq.

29) V. supra, note 25. "For he is the first-born of Joseph" and "the first-born of Manasseh" (17 1) merely emphasize facts and are not meant to explain a privilege. Machir was indeed the first-born and *only son* of Manasseh (v. Gen. 50 23 Nu 26 29) and those who obtained a portion in the Land of Canaan were also the sons of Machir, the father of Gilead. In Josh 17 2 the occupiers of Canaan are called "the remaining sons of Manasseh" after their great-grandfather. But the occupiers of Gilead too are, in v. 6, called "the remaining sons of Manasseh". Ju 5 14 proves that the clans of Manasseh in Canaan as well traced their descent to Machir.

in the region of Tappuach which are mentioned in 17 8-10. For all that, it remains true that the verses are in need of clarification.

We must also reject the view that, in the original version of 16-17, Manasseh preceded Ephraim. The rule is that the author's descriptions run from south to north: Judah, the tribes of Joseph; Simeon, Zebulun-Issachar-Asher, Naphtali. In 17 1-2, too, the author begins his description from the south. Simons's opinion about the structure of 16-17 is correct in general, though it is not possible to follow him in every detail. Cc. 16-17 are a compound description of the entire portion of Joseph together with its two sections. In 17 10 Simons accepts the reading ויהי הים גבולם; but the words ובאשר יפגעון מצפון are themselves sufficient to prove that this verse concludes the description of the joint portion of Ephraim and Manasseh. In 16 5 the author repeats his description of the southern border, already given in vv. 1-3. There is nothing peculiar in this, since he also repeats the description of boundaries in the case of Judah and Benjamin. For some reason unknown to us, in v. 5 he divides the border into two and begins with "Ateroth-addar". But he does the same thing also with the internal border in 16 6 and 17 7-9: he divides it at "Hammichmethath". Thus we see that there is here something typical of the whole description. — As regards the *text* of 16-17, Simons's view is undoubtedly optimistic. Corruptions and omissions have crept into the text, making it really impossible to interpret as it stands (so de Groot, quoted by Simons, p. 192).

First of all, the words ויצא הגבול הימה (16 6) should, without any doubt, be attached to v. 5. But even then it is remarkable that apparently only *half* the border is described here (Ateroth-addar to the sea). The disorder of vv. 6-7 is particularly plain. In these verses there is drawn a line beginning at Hammichmethath in the north and ending at Jericho in the south! The absurdity of this is evident from the end of v. 7: "and it went out at the Jordan". A line which comes down from Hammichmethath and reaches Jericho cuts the Benjamin-Ephraim border and makes a salient shutting off the territory of Ephraim and separating it from the Jordan. *Jericho* would then mark the *end* of Ephraim's border, and the section Jericho — the Jordan would not in any way be a continuation of it. Without any doubt the true verse order has here become distorted through the confusion of similar words and haplography. I restore the following text:

ויהי גבול נחלתם	The border of their inheritance was
מזרחה עטרות אדר עד	on the east side [30] Ateroth-addar
בית חרון עליון, ויצא הגבול	to Upper Beth-horon and the border
הימה. וירד מזרחה עטרות	went out towards the sea. Eastwards [31] it descended to Ataroth [32] and Naarah,
ונערתה ופגע ביריחו ויצא	touched Jericho and came out to the
הירדן.	Jordan.
המכמתת מצפון, ונסב	Hammichmethath on the north, and
הגבול מזרחה תאנת שלה	the border turned eastwards to Taanath-
ועבר אותו ממזרח ינוחה	shiloh and passed it from the east to Ja- noah and it went down from Janoah and
וירד מינוחה ויצא הירדן.	came out to the Jordan. From Tappuach
מתפוח ילך הגבול ימה וגו'.	the border ran westwards etc.

This text provides a complete and intelligible description of the southern and northern borders of Ephraim from the Jordan to the sea. The description starts from the middle of each border and traces the one westwards and eastwards and the other, conversely, eastwards and westwards. The southern border is repeated, but, as is the author's custom in such repetitions, with certain differences. First, the repetition contains an abbreviation. Again, in place of Bethel-Luz, another point is marked — "Naarah"; instead of "the *border* of Lower Beth-horon" (which in fact includes Upper Beth-horon as well) we find another, more precise, southern demarkation — "Upper Beth-horon". In 17 7-10 the author re-traces the western section of the northern boundary, so as to clarify the complex situation in the district of Tappuach and to add an explanation of the line "the valley of Kanah".

---

30) The author begins his dscription on the eastern point of the half-line (Ateroth-addar) and works to the west.

31) Reading מזרחה for מינוחה. Janoah is identical with Jānūn, south-east of Shechem.

32) Identical with Ateroth-addar (v. 5) and with Ataroth in v. 2.

OMISSION OF THE CITY LISTS

It is particularly important to examine the omission in 16 9. The interpreters and translators are obliged to patch up this verse into a complete sentence. The words "this is the portion of the tribe of the Children of Ephraim according to their clans" (8) round off the delineation of the borders. Now comes v. 9 to relate something about "the cities set apart", but — *it does not relate anything!* There is a subject, but no predicate! Next: "*all* the cities" sums up "cities" which have not been listed or even mentioned. The phrase "all the cities" has a parallel in 15 32, only there the total number is given, whereas here there is nothing at all. V. 9 is simply a meaningless, disconnected fragment. The absence of a predicate and of a total number are literary "scars" which bear witness to excisions. The *waw* of והערים indicates that a detailed list of cities had preceded this verse.

From this we may conjecture that, after "this is the portion of the tribe of the Children of Ephraim according to their clans", the original version of Josh contained a *full register of the cities of Ephraim*, just as in Josh 15 20 sqq., and that this was excised in a later edition. This register continued with the words "and the cities set apart for the children of Ephraim in the portion of Manasseh", followed by the *number* of the cities, which has also been omitted. After "all the cities" came, as in 15 32, the combined total of the cities of Ephraim and of the cities set apart, and this number too has been lost[33]. The *names* of the

---

33) For total numbers of cities indicated by כל cf. Josh 20 9 21 19 26 33 37

cities set apart were listed by the author in the parallel description of the portion of Manasseh (17 7-10), which has also suffered excisions in a later edition.

There can be no doubt that the text of 17 9 is also defective. According to this verse (as also 16 8) *the Wadi Kanah* was the boundary between Ephraim and Manasseh, it being explicitly emphasized: "And the border of Manasseh was *on the north* of the Wadi". This being so, no intelligible meaning can be extracted from the words "southwards to the Wadi these cities belonged to Ephraim amongst the cities of Manasseh". For, if the mixed population was *south* of the brook, the author should speak of the cities of *Manasseh* amongst the cities of *Ephraim*, instead of the converse. Simons[34], realizing this, proposes to read:

וירד הגבול נחל קנה	The border descended to the Wadi Kanah
נגבה. 'מצפון' לנחל	southwards. To the north of the brook these
'ה'ערים האלה לאפ-	cities belonged to Ephraim amongst the cities
רים בתוך ערי מנשה.	of Manasseh.

While this emendation removes the chief absurdity, it does not satisfactorily restore the verses. First, the direction Tappuach — the Wadi Kanah is not "southwards", but *westwards*, as is explained in 16 8. Further, the words "these cities" are left hanging (just as "and the cities . . . all the cities" in 16 9), since they are not preceded by any enumeration of cities. The parallel passages in 17 12   19 8 16 23 31 39 48 show that "these cities" always follows a city list[35]. Thus such a list has been excised here and the scar of the operation remains. I assume that we have here textual confusions and omissions of the kind that we found in c. 16. Apparently the cities set apart were in the area of Tappuach and not all along the Wadi Kanah, and the con-

---

38 39. In 21 3 8 a detailing of city numbers begins and ends with the phrase הערים האלה.

34) Structure, pp. 210 sqq.

35) Cf. 21 40. On the other hand, ibid. 3 8, the expression comes at the beginning and the end of a list of city numbers. In any case, the expression is part of the terminology employed in listing cities.

fusion is due to the displacement of the verses. It may be conjectured that after v. 8 came the words ויהיו לאפרים ("and there
belonged to Ephraim"), followed by the list of the cities set apart
which is missing in our version. After the list, the text continued:

הערים האלה לאפרים	These cities belonged to Ephraim amongst
בתוך ערי מנשה. וירד	the cities of Manasseh. And the border des-
הגבול נחל קנה, נגבה	cended to the Wadi Kanah, southwards to
לנחל... לאפרים... וג־	the Wadi... to Ephraim..., and the border of
בול מנשה מצפון לנ־	Manasseh was on the north side of the Wadi,
חל, ויהי תצאותיו הי־	and it went out to the sea. Southwards to
מה. נגבה לאפרים וצ־	Ephraim and northwards to Manasseh, and the
פונה למנשה,ויהי הים	sea was their border. And at Asher etc.
גבולם. ובאשר וגו'.	

The repetition (v. 10) "southwards to Ephraim" etc., is perhaps
meant to stress that there were mixed communities only in the
region of Tappuach, whereas along the Wadi Kanah there was
a clear-cut boundary.

Similarly, it may be conjectured that v. 11 was preceded by
a list of the cities of Manasseh which v. 11 then rounds off
with the enumeration of the unconquered Canaanite cities [36].

The foregoing discussion entitles us to suppose that the extant Book of Joshua is a late Judahite version of the original
book. The Judahite editor, while making no alterations to the
text of the ancient work, was not interested in the detailed city
lists of Ephraim and Manasseh. He left the boundary demarcations,
but excised the lists of cities, and in some places the scars remain clearly recognizable. In a different manner and with greater
carelessness he also abbreviated the descriptions of the portions
of the Galilean tribes. His motive was neither political nor religious, but, if one may say so, publisher-scribe's convenience.

---

36) That cc. 16 and 17 once contained city lists had already been surmised
by Elliger, ZPDV 1930, p. 307, and von Rad: Die Priesterschrift im Hexateuch,
1934, pp. 153-154.

THE CANAANITE ZONE TO THE NORTH OF MANASSEH

C. 17 11 provides an explanation of the fact that the northern border of Manasseh (and of Joseph as a whole) was not marked in detail: all along the northern border from the Jordan to the sea (from Beth-shean to Dor) there ran *Canaanite* territory. Here the list mentions *the cities and their daughters*, as in the case of the Philistine area which stretched all along the western border of Judah (15 45-47). Just as in the case of Judah only the *sea* beyond the Philistine area could be given as the western border-line, so here was it only possible to indicate the border-line of Asher-Issachar, on the other side of the Canaanite territory, as the northern border-line of Manasseh (17 10).

However, the topographical delimitation of the Canaanite zone in 17 11 by the words "and Manasseh had in Issachar and Asher Beth-shean and its daughters" etc., is remarkably perplexing. In what sense was this zone both "part of Manasseh" and "in Issachar and Asher"? The common interpretation of this delineation is that the zone was something like "the cities set apart" of Ephraim "*amidst* the portion of the children of Manasseh" (15 9 17 9). But, in fact, there is no analogy here. The Canaanite territory was a *continuous* region stretching the whole breadth of the Land, and not "separate cities". It is true that, if we accept the identification of *Shihor-libnath*, on the border of Asher (19 26), with Ez-zerqa, then the portion of Asher protruded into this territory. And if we assume that "En-dor" in 17 11 is not a corruption, then the Canaanite territory protruded, at this point, into the portion of Issachar. Still, even assigning this shape to the territory can by no means justify the text of 17 11. Moreover, there are good grounds for questioning the very assumptions made above. The words "and it reacheth to Carmel westward, and to Shihor-libnath" (19 26) mean that the *Carmel* is the end of the *western border* of Asher, and that the border did not reach the sea, but passed through the *Kishon valley*; hence it is in this valley, close to Carmel, that Shihor-libnath (or Shihor and Libnath, following the text of the versions) is to be placed. The line curved round in the region of *Yoqneam*, where it met the border of *Zebulun* [37]. The Canaanite zone of Manasseh was, accordingly, continuous from Dor to Beth-shean. Furthermore, it is clear from Ju 1 27 that En-dor was *not* part of this Canaanite area, and that it should therefore be deleted in Josh 17 11. This means that the zone nowhere protrudes into the portion of Issachar. The borders of Asher and Issachar together form a continous, straightforward line which serves as the northern border of the Canaanite zone.

Attempts have been made to explain the delimitation in 17 11 *historically* and *ethnographically*. According to Alt and Noth [38], the terms used reflect the changes in the ownership of this area. At first the area was considered part of the portion of Asher and Issachar. In the course of time, however, the claim of these tribes to possession was superseded by the claim of Manasseh. The author (or "recensionist") took his information about the change of ownership from Ju 1 27-28 and from his "documents"; and in Josh 17 11 he records the historical passage of the area from tribe to tribe. Simons, too, inclines to this view [39]. Mowinckel [40] proposes a historico-ethnographical explanation. According to this, the author knew, from Ju 1 27-28, that the cities of the area were Canaanite at first, but finally came' under the control of Manasseh. But he also knew — "undoubtedly from living popular tradition" — that the *fellah* population of the district was descended from Asher and Issachar. In 17 11-13 he indicates the historical

---

37) From this point the men of Zebulun used to penetrate into the gulf of Acre, and this is alluded to in Gen 49 13.

38) Alt, Ortsliste, pp. 64-68 ; Noth, Josua, pp. 76 sqq.

39) Structure, pp. 194, 211-213.

40) Josua 13-19, pp. 28-30.

vicissitudes and the ethnographic heterogeneity of the territory.

Unfortunately, these explanations are completely unwarranted by the text.

The meaning of 17 11-12 is solely *geographical*: the verses have *no historical significance*. There is no reference to a *change* of ownership. There is no mention of the fact that the district *belonged* first to Asher and Issachar and then *passed* into the control of Manasseh. The passage of a portion from one tribe to another is nowhere recorded in Josh. The district belongs *simply and solely* "to Manasseh", only, in a certain geographical sense, its position is defined by the words ביששכר ובאשר. Similarly, there is no reference to *an ethnographically heterogeneous* population in the district. On the contrary, the population is descri-bed as entirely *homogeneous*, viz: there is no ethnological di-stinction between city-dwellers and fellahin: *they are all Canaanites*. The cities and "their daughters" alike are all Canaanite. The population includes neither city-dwellers of Manasseh nor fellahin of Asher and Issachar, seeing that it contains no Israelite ele-ment at all.

The confusion has been caused by a mistaken interpretation of the words ביששכר ובאשר. These do not mean *in* Issachar and *in* Asher, hut *beside* Issachar and *beside* Asher — *along* their portion. For this use of ב cf. 1 Sam 29 1 Ez 10 15. In Josh 17 10 it is related that Ephraim and Manasseh "touched" Asher and Issachar to the north. The end of v. 11 adds that all along the area of "contact" runs Canaanite territory. Here too, the boun-daries are conceived as *fixed, definite lines*, allowing for no ex-changes or transitions. This is nothing more or less than a de-scription of the situation in the actual period of the Conquest: on the northern border of Manasseh there is a Canaanite zone which cuts it off from Asher and Issachar along the whole length of the border.

And not only the delimitation of the border, but all that is related in 17 12-18 (which is not a composite collection, but a *homogeneous story*) reflects the situation of this period. The end of v. 12 describes the character of the zone and explains why it is Canaanite: the children of Manasseh were not able to drive out these Canaanites. The reason is given in vv. 16 and 18: the

Canaanites had iron chariots. This fixes the date as *the beginning of the Conquest*, when the iron chariot was still militarily decisive. V. 13 refers not to the period of the Kingdom, but to a somewhat later stage in the wars of Conquest. When the tribes of Israel became firmly established in the Land, they made the Canaanites tributaries, but did not drive them out. However, this was only a temporary solution of the problem. The children of Joseph conceived the urge *to expel* the Canaanites, instead of being satisfied with the tributary agreement. According to this story, the agitation for expulsion arose while Joshua was still alive. The children of Joseph complained that they were cramped in their portion, because the mountain was covered with forests and the valley occupied by the Canaanites with their iron chariots. Joshua proposed to them two courses of action: to clear the forest on the mountain, and to expel the Canaanites in the valley, despite their iron chariots [41]. The expulsion of the

---

41) In 17 11-18 there is no duplication or contradiction or combination of sources, nor is there any allusion to the migration of the Children of Manasseh into Transjordania. The analyses of the critics (cf., e. g., the Commentaries of Steuernagel and Noth) dismember a continuous story which describes in a natural and vivid way an exchange of views between peasants and their leader. Vv. 14-18 form the *continuation* of 11-13 and are not to be separated from them. Vv. 11-13 relate that the Emeq was held by the Canaanites and that the Israelites, even when they grew strong, could not drive them out; while vv. 14-18 contain Joshua's dying instructions to expel the Canaanites from the Emeq. The claim of the Children of Joseph that they are overcrowded and should therefore be given an additional "lot" is met by Joshua, first with the instruction to clear the forest, if Mount Ephraim in its wooded state is too confined for them. The Children of Joseph counter that the mountain will not be large enough for them, even if they clear it of forest. True, the Emeq is within their territory but it is occupied by the Canaanites equipped with iron chariots. Joshua's reply to this is that they must perform both tasks: clear the forest and expel the Canaanites, thus obtaining additional agricultural land and doubling their "lot". In v. 18 it is only necessary to read חזק אתה (or חזקה ממנו with the LXX) instead of חזק הוא. The verse then explains v. 17: since your numbers are great you can gain what is virtually a second

Canaanites ended with the war of *Sisera*. In Josh 17, however, the valley is still entirely Canaanite. Here too we have a description and a story of extremely archaic character.

lot, "for" the mountain will be yours (as fertile soil), despite its forests, if you clear it; "for" you will expel the Canaanites, despite their iron chariots, because you are strong. The word כי has here two meanings. — The forest and the mountain in v. 15 are the same as in v. 18. V. 15 likewise contains no allusion to Transjordania, for there were "Rephaim" in the Land of Canaan too. In Gen 15 20 the *Perizzites and the Rephaim* are mentioned together amongst the peoples of Canaan, just as in our v. 15. "Emeq Rephaim" is close to Jerusalem. Cf. also 2 Sam 21 15-22

THE LIST OF LEVITICAL CITIES. AN ANCIENT UTOPIA

The story of *the Levitical cities* (21) completes the narrative of the distribution of the Land. This story too bears an extremely archaic and utopian stamp.

Chapter 21 belongs to the source P. It is therefore considered as post-exilic and, according to accepted opinion, one of the latest additions to P. This chapter has been interpreted as an expression of the — fantastic and unrealistic — demand by the post-exilic Priesthood for a territorial portion. The author of the chapter, while modelling himself on Ezekiel (45 1-5 48 8-14), is obliged, on Wellhausen's interpretation [42], to adopt "archaic trimmings" and to ignore *Jerusalem* and the Temple — no less! There is no doubt that this interpretation is wrong.

Such a dating makes it quite impossible to explain the absence of Jerusalem from the list of the cities of the Priests and Levites. A priestly demand for a territorial portion in the time of the Second Temple could not have ignored Jerusalem, no matter how unrealistic the demand or how archaic the disguise which it required. To demand Shechem, Gezer, Taanach, Gibbethon, Rehov, etc., while ignoring Jerusalem — this is simply a puerile game of blind-man's-buff. Nor is it only Jerusalem that is missing; the truth is that practically the *whole territory of Judah* of the Persian period has been omitted. Of the *Levitical* cities not one is in the territory of Judah (except Beth-horon — if at that time it belonged to Judah). All the *priestly* cities in Judah's portion were part of the then state of Edom: from Hebron southwards (21 13-16). Only the four priestly cities in the portion

---

42) Wellhausen, Prolegomena zur Geschichte Israels [6], pp. 153-158.

of Benjamin belonged to the territory of Judah[43]. It is out of the question to suppose that such a "programme" could have expressed any "demand" whatever on the part of the Priesthood of the Second Temple[44].

That the list is not of post-exilic provenance follows from this further consideration: the *Levites* are allotted thirty five cities, and the Priests only thirteen. At the time of the Second Temple there were very few Levites, whereas the Priests ran into many thousands. Hence the section about the Levitical cities is just as archaic, out-of-date and unsuited to contemporary conditions as all the rest of the legislation of P concerning the Priests and Levites was in the time of the Second Temple.

S. Klein sought to prove that Josh 21 is an ancient register of *actual* Priestly and Levitical settlements which was drawn up in the reign of *David*. The register assumes the unity of all the Israelite tribes and the inclusion of the Canaanite and Philistine cities (Gezer, Gibbethon, etc.) within the confines of the Kingdom of Israel. In support of this view it is pointed out that the list contains several cities which we know, from other sources, to have possessed shrines and to have served as places of residence for Priests or Levites: Hebron, Gibeon, Anathoth, Shechem,

---

43) Cf. Noth, Josua, pp. 100-101. Noth expresses even the view that Josh 21 lists just those cities in which Levitical families from outside the autonomous Judah of the Persian time dwelt — i. e. families from "the Diaspora". But it is obvious that in c. 21 the settlements of *all* the Levitical and Priestly families are meant. Similarly, Noth's statement (ibid.) that cities from the state of *Samaria* are entirely missing from the list is not correct. *Shechem* is specifically mentioned, *Kibzaim* is certainly in Samaria too, and perhaps *Beth-horon* as well.

44) Pfeiffer, Introduction to the O. T., pp. 308-309, gives it as his opinion that Josh 21 is from the pen of a Levite of the 3rd century, who, as a protest against the denial of a portion to the Priests and Levites, assigned them 48 cities on paper. Pfeiffer places these cities "all in the vicinity of Jerusalem". This is certainly a very sensible geographic amendment of the supposed Levite's "protest". The only flaw in it is that Pfeiffer's amendment never occured to the Levite himself.

Tabor and others[45]. Albright too reached a similar conclusion. He tries to show that the register is not earlier than *Saul* and not later than *Solomon*, and that the time which fits it best is the reign of *David*. The policy of organizing the settlement of the Priests and Levites remained, it is true, "an ideal programme". But it is based on the actual experiment of David in creating a new administrative organization of the Israelite tribes[46].

But this dating too splinters on the granite fact of *Jerusalem's* absence from the list. David brought the ark up to Jerusalem and planned to make the city a political and religious centre. Solomon built the Temple there. Zadok and Abiathar dwelt there. How, then, is it conceivable that they should have forgotten to include Jerusalem in the programme? Again, if the programme had been based, to any extent at all, on the formation of *actual* settlements, how would it have been possible to forget not only Jerusalem, but also *Shiloh, Nob, Bethel, Gilgal, Mizpah, Dan, Beersheba, Rama* — cities which possessed shrines and priests? And how could *Shechem* have been given to the Levites, and not to the Priests?

Moreover, this whole programme stems from *P's conception of the Priests and Levites*. It takes for granted the absolute division, both genealogical and functional, between Priests and Levites which we find in P. Nay more — it carries this division to its *extreme*: it would embody it in a *territorial* segregation. It settles the Priests and Levites in *separate communities*. Even those who consider P early must concede that the absolute separation between Priests and Levites was, in early times, no more than a utopian *demand* on the part of the Aharonic priests which was not actually realized. In the stories about David and Solomon in the Books of Samuel and Kings there is no mention that they endeavoured to effect a separation between Priests and Levites. Much less is there any mention of an attempt to embody it in the form of separate settlement[47]. Indeed, as long as the *bamoth*

---

45) V. Klein, ערי הכהנים והלויים וערי המקלט (קבץ החברה העברית לחקירת א"י ועתיקותיה, תרצ"ה), pp. 81 sqq. 93 sqq. Cf. Löhr, Asylwesen in Alten Testament (1930), p. 34.

46) Albright, Archaeology and the Religion of Israel, 1942, pp. 121-129.

47) Polemizing against "the current critical theory" about the Priests and

were in existence, an actual programme of settling Priests and Levites in *separate* communities could never have been thought of. In so far as Priests and Levites officiated, in early times, in the sanctuaries, they were divided in *function*, but associated in *the place of their officiation* — in the sanctuaries. They could have been accommodated in separate *quarters*: but how could they have been settled in separate *cities*? In such circumstances, how could they have performed their duty in the sanctuaries? What sense would there have been, for example, in settling only Priests in *Jutta*, and only Levites in *Shechem*? In the time of David and Solomon sanctuaries and bamoth existed everywhere and the Priests and Levites must have resided *where they worked* and utterly opposed any "programme" of separate communities in special cities. Both alike were interested in obtaining "plots" in every city which contained a sanctuary.

There is a further point. The "programme" of Josh 21 gives a most peculiar form to the territorial segregation of Priests and Levites: it divides the whole land into *two* regions along the Ephraim-Dan border. North of this line it settles all the Levites, and south of it all the Priests. From Dan to Gezer and Eltheke not a priest lives! How is it conceivable that such a "programme" has any connection with an actual experiment in organization, or that it embodies anything real at all? It should be noted that neither in Josh nor in the Torah is there any mention of or reference to the division of Priests and Levites into wards (serving by turns). This makes the "programme" utterly fictitious.

The unrealistic and utopian character of Josh 21 is made particularly evident by the list of the Levitical cities of *Dan* (23-24). This list included *Eltheke* and *Gibbethon* which were undoubtedly

Levites, Albright maintains (ibid. pp. 125 sqq.) that the temple psalmody is ancient and that there are good grounds for supposing that David did actually organize the order of Levitical singers. However, this question is not really relevant to our purpose. First of all, no order of singers is mentioned either in the Pentateuch or in Josh. Secondly, for our purpose it would be necessary to prove that David wanted to give substance to the *exclusive* privilege of the Priests as laid down by P. Of this there is no proof.

always Philistine cities (v. 1 Ki 15 27 16 15). True, David conquered these cities too [48]; but the conquests of David were *political* and exchanges of population were just what they did not involve. So *Gezer*, though within his kingdom, remained Canaanite (v. 1 Ki 9 16). Quite apart from all this, Josh 21 actually contains no mention of the political position in the time of David and Solomon. According to the list, Eltheke, Gibbethon, Ayalon and Gath-rimmon are cities in *the portion of Dan* — that portion which according to 19 47, *was not the real territory of Dan* ! It follows that the author explicitly regards these Levitical cities as "utopian" and unreal. He consistently follows the description of the portions in 19 40-48 where the territory distributed does not include the northern portion of Dan. Since Dan, ideally, has no portion in the north, the author "gives" the Levites cities in its unreal portion. This can be understood only in the context of the historical situation *prior to* the creation of Dan's northern portion. But how can it be explained in a later context? Is it possible that David would have drawn up such a programme? Can we suppose that he would have exempted the northern Dan from the obligation imposed on the other tribes, while transferring this obligation to its southern ghost? Conversely, could David have wished that in the northern portion of Dan there should be neither Priests nor Levites living? Obviously the "programme" does not suit any late date. In any later programme it would have been impossible to treat *the city of Dan*, where the family of *Jonathan ben Gershom* lived, as if it were non-existent and to break off from "the portion of Dan" cities in the Philistine area. Again, the inclusion of Gezer amongst the Levitical cities proves that the list is not of Davidic date, seeing that Gezer remained a *Canaanite* city till the reign of Solomon. Solomon rebuilds it (1 Ki 9 16-27), but does not settle Levites there.

We are therefore on firm ground in asserting that the list of Priestly and Levitical cities in Josh 21 constitutes a *utopia*. But since it cannot be a post-exilic utopia it must of necessity be an *ancient Priestly utopia* which could have been put into words

48) Albright, ibid. p. 121.

only at *the beginning* of the period of the Conquest, *before* the shrines and bamoth were established in the settlements of Israel. The motif of this utopia is the special idea of P, as formulated in Lev 17 and particularly in the remarkable story in Josh 22 9-34. The idea of *the unification of the cultus* does appear in P, but P's conception of this cultic unity is entirely different from D's, as has been observed above. P does not forbid the *bamoth*, but it does forbid the offering of sacrifices on *field-altars* where there is no shrine. Neither in Lev 17 nor in Josh 22 is anything said about the plurality of *shrines*. In Josh 22 the Transjordanian tribes build not a shrine, but an *altar*, and the community regards this as a treacherous sin on their part against the Tent of Meeting. The antiquity of the story is vouched for by its still considering Transjordania as *unclean ground* (19). As a matter of fact, there is in existence only one shrine — the Tent of Meeting; and this it is that sanctifies the Land and makes it "a land in the possession of Jahweh". The writer of the story thinks of the portable tent with no fixed abode as *the sole shrine* of Israel for the future too. The establishment of shrines in all the settlements of Israel, after the pattern of the Tent, is still beyond his ken. This idea, which was current in Priestly circles at the time of the Conquest, is also the source of the settlement programme for the tribe of Levi. The purpose of this programme is *not* to organize *the employment of the whole tribe of Levi* in the Tent of Meeting. It has no connection with a programme of officiation *by wards* (or shifts). Its real purpose is rather *to break* the actual link between the tribe and the service of the Tent. The office of *guarding* the Tent came to an end with the distribution of the Land of Canaan amongst the tribes. The cultus of the single Tent could not support the whole tribe. Hence P, while maintaining the tribe's right to the sacrificial gifts, is at pains to provide it with a supplementary source of livelihood and to give it possession of "cities" with plots for cattle-rearing. For P the functions of the Priesthood are principally functions *outside* the Tent. The Priests are the teachers of the Law, the authorities in matters of impurity and purity, etc. Apparently the author imagined the service of the Tent as assigned, in practice, to one of the families, the whole tribe ideally having the right to participate in it — much as in Deut 18 6-8. For this reason, his territorial programme for the tribe of Levi nowhere takes into account officiation in the Tent. This programme has no parallel. The author drew it up in accordance with the idea of the complete segregation of Priests from Levites. This idea is the reason for his settling Priests and Levites in two separate "lands": one entirely Priestly and the other entirely Levitical. The programme has no connection at all with those cities which subsequently became cultic centres.

This Priestly programme remained utopian and no attempt was ever made to implement it. Its basic conceptions were held at an early time in certain Priestly circles, but did not gain general acceptance. The complete segregation of Priests from Levites did not carry the day, at that time. Nor was the unification of the cultus in the Tent realized. With the establishment of numerous shrines in the Land the cultus became a source of livelihood for many families of Priests and Levites. Families of Levites, on being absorbed into the shrines, were transformed into families of Priests. Neither Priests nor Levites could or would have obtained territory in accordance with the programme. They settled wherever there were shrines. In the time of the Second Temple, the ethnographic and political situation made it impossible to put the archaic programme into practice. Hence this programme remained an obsolete, literary utopia, a memorial to the aspirations of the Priesthood at the time of the Conquest. Its date is fixed by the missing of the northern portion of Dan, viz: before Dan's northward migration [49].

49) Albright, ibid. pp. 122-123, argues that the list of Levitical cities is somewhat later than the boundary list, since in it *Shechem* of Manasseh is already considered as a city of Ephraim (20 7 21 21) and *Heshbon* of Reuben (13 17) as a city of Gad (21 37). This last difference is particularly instructive, in that it hints at the process of Reuben's degeneration and Gad's expansion into its portion — a process which had been completed by the time of *Mesha* (9th Cent.). — But Shechem and Heshbon are both *border-cities* (17 7, cf. 16 6; 13 17 26), and fluctuations of border-cities are to be found both in the boundary lists and in the city lists throughout Josh (v. supra). Hence no proof of a late historical process can be adduced from this. 1 Chr 6 63-64 shows us that this list assumes that Reuben is still in existence and in occupation of its cities.

THE IDEAL AND UTOPIAN LAND OF ISRAEL

Throughout the Pentateuch, Josh and Ju runs *an unreal utopian conception* of *the Land of Israel* — this is a fact which the Higher Criticism could not ignore. But it has obstinately sought *to blur* this conception and *to obscure* its *character and origin*. Herein lies one of its great failures. The Higher Criticism has endeavoured to avoid recognizing that the aforesaid conception is a *purely utopian idea* which cannot be explained either by the *real ethnic settlement* of the tribes, or by the *real political development* of the Kingdom of Israel. Because of its dogmatic assumptions, the Higher Criticism has refused to recognize that here we have a utopian idea of *ancient date which preceded* alike the Conquest and the establishment of the Kingdom.

Alt saw that in the boundary list of Joshua, as in the list of gaps in the Conquest in Ju 1 27-35, there is a "theoretical" element and that these passages give expression to a juridical claim to ownership of *all* the Land, from the Jordan to the sea and from the River of Egypt to the Ladder of Tyre, including areas which were not conquered. The boundary list apportions the *entire* Land amongst the tribes, without leaving an inch of ground unoccupied. In Alt's view, this theoretically complete apportionment gave expression to the claims of the tribes as formulated in the period of the Judges[50]. However, this interpretation is undoubtedly mistaken. Separate claims by *tribes* could not have combined to form such a "theoretical" unbroken territory, di-

50) Alt, Landnahme, pp. 26 sqq; Stammesgrenzen, pp. 13—19.

vided into tribal portions by such uniform boundary lines. Again, Dan in fact had already renounced its old portion in the early days of the Conquest. But in the boundary list its "claim" is preserved untouched. Indeed, the *real* portion of Dan in the north is not included in the boundary list! No wonder Alt tries "to delete" Dan completely[51], seeing that its two portions present a snag for the theory. But it is really necessary "to delete" *Asher* as well. For how can it be supposed that the small tribe of Asher had a "claim" to receive the territory of Tyre and Sidon — something that even *David and Solomon* never dreamt of? Obviously, the "theoretical" element in the apportionment of the Land cannot be explained by the aspirations of the tribes.

But it is not the conception of the Land in Josh 13-19 alone which cannot be explained "realistically", either by the process of the Conquest or by later developments in the time of the Kingdom. The same applies to the conception of the Land found throughout Josh, as also to that found in the Pentateuch and Ju 1-3. It is not correct to say, as Alt does, that in Josh there is a programme "of complete conquest of the settled area in Palestine"[52], or, in Mowinckel's words, that there is an idea — originating in *David's* time — of the greater Land of Israel "from the River of Egypt to the Ladder of Tyre"[53]. The ideal Land has boundaries at once much *wider* and much *narrower* than these — boundaries which conform neither to those of "the settled area in Palestine" nor to those of David's or Solomon's kingdom.

In the Bible we find *five* different conceptions of the *Land of Israel* corresponding to changes in the historical situation, viz: 1. The Land of Canaan, or the Land of the Patriarchs; 2. Moses' Land of Israel; 3. Joshua's Land of Israel; 4. The Land of the real Israelite Settlement; 5. The Kingdom of Israel. The first four conceptions are *ethnographic*, the fifth *imperialistic*.

---

51) Stammesgrenzen, p. 18. His own wish to "erase" Dan Alt finds without any reason in Ju I 34-35.

52) Alt, Josua, p. 15 sqq.

53) Mowinckel, Josua 13-19, pp. 16-17, 24.

THE LAND OF CANAAN

The Land destined for Israel in the Pentateuch, from Gen 12 to Nu 26, is *the Land of Canaan*, which had been promised to the Patriarchs. The *borders* of this territory are: from the Jordan on the east to the sea on the west, and from the Wadi of Egypt (or from the Sea of Suf, or the desert, or the "River of Egypt") in the south to the Euphrates, or the Gateway to Hamath, in the north (Gen 15 18 Ex 23 31 Nu 13 21 34 2-12 Deut 1 7 3 25 11 24 Josh 1 4 13 1-6 Ju 3 3; cf. Ez 47 15-20, also Gen 10 19)[54].

54) The term used for the most northern of all the border delimitations is "the River Euphrates". A close approximation to this is "up to the Gateway to Hamath" (לבוא חמח). True, the border "up to the Gateway to Hamath" is not "a clear line". But that does not leave its meaning in any doubt: at the entrance to the country of Hamath, in the vicinity of Hamath. (For the expression לבוא cf. 1 Chr 5 9: "unto the entering in of the wilderness"; 2 Chr 26 8; "to the entering in of Egypt"; Gen 24 62 10 19 30 13 10 1 Ki 18 46, et al.). This meaning is made plain by the parallel expression "the border of Hamath", Ez 47 16-17, and by the expression "beside Hamath", ibid. 48 1. — It is particularly far-fetched of Noth to propose that "up to the Gateway to Hamath" indicates the northern border of *eastern Transjordania*, v. ZDPV 1935, pp. 242 sqq; Comm. to Josh, p. 49. From Nu 13 21 it is clear that the place in fact marks the northern border of *western* Transjordania, since the spies were sent to explore only this territory. Noth has no hesitation in maintaining that Nu 34 7-12 is based on a "document" describing the northern border of *eastern Transjordania* (ZDPV 1935, pp. 239 sqq.), only the "editor" confused east and west and used the "document" (which Noth has never seen!) to describe the

This Land of Canaan includes Lebanon, the territory of Tyre, Sidon, Gebal and "the land of the Philistines". But it does *not* include *Transjordania*. In the boundary list in Nu 34 and in Ez 47 the *Jordan* is the eastern boundary of the Land of Canaan. Moreover, this is the dominant conception in the Pentateuch and in Josh. Gen 13 relates that Lot chose the plain of the Jordan to the east, while Abraham remained in the west — "in the Land of Canaan" (10-18). The Patriarchs roam on the west of the Jordan, traversing the length and breadth of the Land. This is the land on which Jacob "lay" and which was given to him (Gen 28 13). But the Patriarchs do not dwell in *Transjordania*. Jacob merely *passes through* it on his way (32 2-3 32), or lodges there temporarily (33 17). The *Jordan* is the boundary between his native land and foreign soil (31 3 32 10-11). The spies explore only the western territory (Nu 13). The tribes of Israel by-pass Edom, Moab and Ammon and would *pass through* the country of Sihon in order to reach the Land of Canaan by way of Jordan (Nu 20 14—22 1 Deut 2-3). Only the country on the west of Jordan is the Land which Jahweh swore to give to them (Nu 20 12 24 27 12 32 7-12 33 51-53 35 10 Deut 4 26 7 1 8 1 9 1-6 Josh 1 2 5 6, et al.). The request of Gad and Reuben for a portion in Transjordania was regarded as a treacherous rebellion (Nu 32). Transjordania is not part of "the Land in Jahweh's possession": indeed, it is considered "unclean" (Josh 22 19).

The population of "the land of Canaan" was ethnologically very mixed. *Twenty peoples* are listed in it, in various combinations. Eleven are mentioned in Gen 10 15-18. Ten, including *four* not in the first list, are mentioned in Gen 15 19-21. Of these, seven appear in Deut 7 1: the Hittites, Girgashites, Amorites,

---

north of *western Transjordania*. The same happened also in Ez 47 15-18. In other words, we have to suppose that the editor took the description of a border that starts "from *the great sea*" and then turns and comes down towards *the Sea of Kinnereth* as the demarkation of the northern (and western) border of *eastern* Transjordania! — For the expression "to the Gateway to Hamath" in 1 Ki 8 65 2 Ki 14 25 Am 6 14 v. infra, p. 54.

Canaanites, Perizzites, Hivvites and Jebusites; and of these seven, six are named in Ex 23 23 34 11 Deut 20 17. In numerous passages there is special mention of the Canaanites and Amorites. To these fifteen must be added: Amalek (Gen 14 7 Nu 13 29 14 25 43 45), the Geshurites (Josh 13 2 1 Sam 27 8), the Avvim (Josh 13 3 Deut 2 23), Anakim (Nu 13 22 28 33 Deut 1 28 9 2 Josh 11 21-22 14 12 15 Ju 1 10 20), Caphtor-Philistines (Deut 2 23 cf. Gen 21 22-34 26 1-31 Ex 13 17). It would appear that, in the period of the Conquest, the six peoples mentioned in Ex and Nu (leaving out Amalek) constituted the chief national groupings of the inhabitants. The rest were "national dust", culturally indistinguishable from the Canaanite element. The Land of Canaan of the Patriarchal and Conquest periods is characterized by the absence of the *Philistines* of the five principalities (the Philistine pentapolis). The *ancient* Philistines (the Caphtorim) mentioned in the Patriarchal narratives are settled in *Gerar* and the neighbourhood of *Beersheba*. Their relations with the Patriarchs are governed by a treaty of alliance and a treaty of friendship. They are not presented as a military people: the chronicles of *Joshua's wars* (Josh 1-11) *contain no mention whatsoever of the Philistines*. In Josh 11 it is the *Anakim*, not the Philistines, who inhabit Gaza, Gath and Ashdod. The *later* Philistines, those founders of the pentapolis who were distinguished for their military power and who made vassals of the tribes of Israel, do not exist in the ancient Land of Canaan. The commandment of extirpation or expulsion was directed against the seven Canaanite peoples, whereas the subsequent chief enemy of Israel, the Philistines, were not included in it

This Land of Canaan, promised to Israel from the days of the Patriarchs, is conceived as the future ethnic territory of Israel. The promise associated with it is purely *ethnic*, not *imperialistic*. The Land was given to the Israelites as their *home*, and not for them to *rule over* its peoples. The Israelites were commanded to *expel* or *extirpate* the peoples of the Land of Canaan: they were not to let them remain in the land, nor make any treaty with them — not even a treaty of tributary vassalage (Ex 23 23 27-33 34 11-16 Nu 34 51-56 Deut 7 1-5 17-26 9 1-3 11 22-25). They might subdue and make tributaries of dis-

The Land of the Patriarchs

tant nations, but not the nations of the Land of Canaan (Deut 20 10-18). It is true that the Land is to be conquered little by little, piece by piece, but the stages of conquest are determined solely by the *ethnic* power of the Israelites in *dispossessing* the peoples and *occupying* their place (Ex 23 29-30 Deut 7 22). There are only stages of *dispossession*, without any transitional stage of imperialistic rule. Such a promise of imperialistic rule is found, in the Pentateuch, only in relation to peoples outside the Land of Canaan (Gen 25 23 27 29 37 Nu 24 17-18 Deut 28 1 33 17 29). Nor is that all. In the Pentateuch the Land of Canaan is conceived as a country which, at the time of its distribution amongst the tribes, shall have been *completely wrested* from the Canaanites. Nu 34 ordains the distribution amongst the tribes of *the whole* of Canaan, from the Wadi of Egypt to the Gateway to Hamath. The territory of each tribe is reckoned in proportion to *the whole* Land. The Pentateuch does not know of an allotment of only a part of the Land of Canaan.

MOSES' LAND OF ISRAEL

Starting with Nu·21 21-35 we find notices in the ancient books of the formation of a new conception: the *Greater Land of Israel*, the borders of which do not conform to those of the Promised Land. This story, as also Nu 32 Deut 2-3, reflects the discrepancy between the ancient promise and the actual situation. The real conquest of the national territory was not in accord with the idea. At the very outset the tribes conquer territory which they had not intended to conquer, territory which was not part of the Land of Canaan and had not been promised to the Patriarchs—*Transjordania*. This conquest was at first regarded as a temporary prelude to the storming of the Promised Land. In Nu 26 all the tribes muster for war and prepare to take possession of the Land of Canaan and to divide it amongst themselves by lot (52-56). It is only in Nu 32 that Reuben and Gad put before Moses their request that, instead of leading them across the Jordan, he should assign them Transjordania as their possession. Moses flies into a rage and threatens the whole people with the wrath of the Lord. But, after Reuben and Gad undertake to cross over in battle array in the van of the Israelites and to take part in the conquest of Canaan, he gives them Transjordania. The two tribes are later joined by half the tribe of Manasseh which conquers the territory of Gilead. In this way there comes into being the conception of the Greater Land of Israel of Moses' days, embracing the conquered Transjordania and the about to be conquered Canaan. Thus Moses gave the Israelites possession of territory which had not been promised to the Patriarchs. Already in Nu 34 the Land of Canaan is destined to only nine and a half tribes and only ten chiefs are appointed for the distribution of the Land by lot.

Moses' Land of Israel

JOSHUA'S LAND OF ISRAEL

However, the Greater Land of Israel too remained a conception devoid of reality. The occupation of the Land at the
time of the Conquest did not conform to the idea. The wars
of conquest give rise to *Joshua's Land of Israel* — the prevailing
conception from Josh 1 — Ju 3. Joshua's Land is made up of
various elements. There is first the Greater Land of Israel, including both Transjordania and Canaan. Only here Transjordania
is an area the whole of which has been conquered and divided,
whereas Joshua's Canaan falls into several sections. The Land
of Canaan of the Pentateuch is a *single* territorial unit, destined
to the conquered *in its entirety* and to be apportioned *in its
entirely* (from the Wadi of Egypt to the Gateway to Hamath),
as a single unit amongst the tribes. Nu 34 does not mention
any part of the Land of Canaan which was not apportioned by
lot to the tribes. It is otherwise with Joshua's Canaan. Here
there is a part which was not only not conquered, *but was not
even apportioned* amongst the tribes: from Baal Gad in the valley
of the Lebanon to the Gateway to Hamath. A second part is
formed by the territory from Baal Gad to the Negev: this is
the Land allotted to the tribes. But even in this allotted territory
there are areas which were *apportioned*, but not *conquered*: all
the costal strip (Josh 13 2-4), all the Emeq (17 11-12 Ju 1 27),
almost all the portion of Dan (19 47 Ju 1 34-35 18 1-29), Jerusalem, Gezer and other cities (Josh 15 63; 16 10; Ju 1 21 29-33).
The *allotted* Land included *Transjordania*, but not the northern
territory of *Dan*. Thus Joshua's Land of Israel is made up of
three "countries": one conquered and allotted, a second allotted

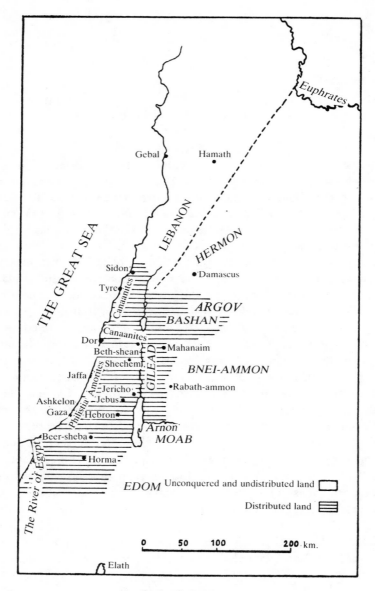

Joshua's Land

but not conquered, and a third neither allotted nor conquered.

In Joshua's Land a most significant *ethnographical* change takes place: after Joshua's wars the *Philistines* of the pentapolis make their appearance. In Josh 11 22 the Philistine cities are still inhabited by the *Anakim*. But by Josh 13 3 they belong to the Philistine rulers (cf. Ju 3 3).

Joshua's Land is a *dynamic* territorial unit, the boundaries of which are considered as *temporary*. The conception of this Land too is *ethnic* and not *imperialistic*, though it is true that it displays features which are not found in the classical Land of Canaan. In it there comes into being a special class of *enslaved* Canaanites — *the Gibeonites*. The territory divided amongst the tribes contains Canaanite enclaves, autonomous, but at the same time tributary (Josh 16 10   17 13   Ju 1 28-30 33 35). This situation, however, is regarded as temporary. The ultimate goal is the *expulsion* of these Canaanites (Josh 17 18). More than that, an integral part of the conception of Joshua's land is the demand for the expulsion not only of the Canaanites in *the apportioned territory*, but also of those in the area *not allocated to the tribes* — from Baal Gad to the Gateway to Hamath (Josh 13 1-6   23 1-13   Ju 2 1-5 20 — 3 4) — that is to say: the demand for the realization of the ideal of the Greater Land of Israel. It is this demand which constitutes Joshua's *national legacy*.

THE REAL LAND OF ISRAEL

As a result of the wars in the period of the Judges there took shape the real Land of Israel as the area of *ethnic Israelite settlement* on both sides of the Jordan. This conception too, of course, is *ethnic* and not imperialistic. *Dan* established itself in the north, beyond the confines of the Land apportioned by Joshua. In the war against *Sisera* the Canaanite Emeq was conquered. The tribes' impulse towards *ethnic expansion* actually petered out. Since the conquered territory was large enough for them, they felt no national economic need to expel the Canaanites and thus complete the conquest of Canaan. *David*, though conquering the Philistine country, does not drive out the Philistines. He is on good terms with *Tyre*. He does not extend the boundaries of *ethnic settlement* either westwards or northwards. David conquers *Jerusalem* for reasons of internal politics, but he is not interested in even ending the autonomy of *Gezer*. Thus the real Land of Israel is a *static* ethnic area with a clearly determined shape. Its borders are entirely new, being neither those of the ideal "Land of Canaan", nor yet those of the Land of Joshua. Its full extent is marked by the new expression "*from Dan to Beersheba*" which appears for the first time in Ju 20 1. At a later date the expression "from the Gateway to Hamath to the Wadi of Egypt", or "to the Sea of the Arabah", was also used sometimes (1 Ki 8 65 2 Ki 14 25 Am 6 14). But this is no more than poetical archaizing, an echo of ancient phraseology. Even in *Solomon's* reign, Israel is settled only "from Dan to Beersheba" (1 Ki 5 5).

THE ISRAELITE EMPIRE

With the establishment of *David's kingdom* something new comes into being: the *Israelite Empire* is created. This is neither the Land of Canaan nor the Greater Land of Israel. The nucleus of this Empire is the *real* Land of Israel, the clearly determined ethnic area, but its boundaries stretch out further. To the real Land of Israel there are added, on the west, east and north, new regions — not as areas of ethnic Israelite settlement, but as provinces of *imperialist rule*: the coast, Edom, Moab, Ammon, Aram. These borders have nothing to do with the ancient "Land of Canaan". The Empire does not aspire to fulfil the national legacy of Joshua by completing the conquest of the Land of Canaan, for it includes neither Tyre, Sidon nor Lebanon, nor does it seek to push forward its northern border to Hamath or the Euphrates. Conversely, it does include not only Transjordania, but even regions which were both outside the limits of Israelite settlement and outside the ideal Land of Canaan: Edom, Moab, Ammon, Aram. The imperial rule took various forms in these countries. While Philistia was annexed by David to his Kingdom (as apparently also Edom), Moab and Aram were only tributary vassals (2 Sam 8).

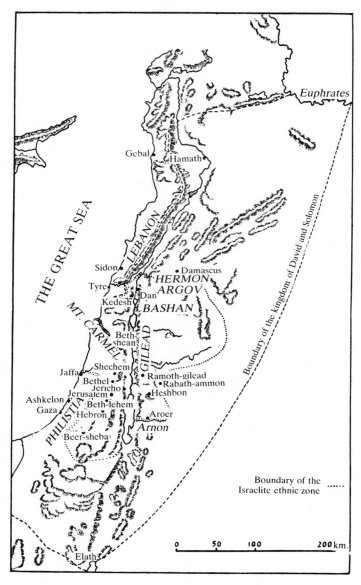

The Kingdom of David and Solomon

THE LAND OF CANAAN — AN ANCIENT UTOPIA

From what has been said it is obvious how superficial are the current explanations of the fixing of the borders of Canaan on the Euphrates or in the proximity of Hamath. These borders are not "patriotic dreams" of "later times", nor are they in any way connected with *David's* rule in Aram (2 Sam 8) or with Solomon's rule beyond the River from Tiphsah to Gaza (1 Ki 5 4) [55].

The "patriotic dreams" of later times, the Messianic visions, are known to us. The hope of conquering all "the Land of Canaan" to the Euphrates is no part of the Messianic vision, but it does contain the hope that "sons will return to their border" (Jer 31 16), to the *real* Land of Israel. No prophet envisages the occupation of Tyre, Sidon, Gebal up to the Euphrates. In Ob 19 there is a prophecy that the Israelites will possess the *Mountain of Esau* which is *outside* the Land of Canaan. Much less do the "patriotic dreams" constrict the border of Israel on the *west* or forgo their claim to Transjordania (cf. Jer 49 1-2 Ob 19 Zech 10 10). The ancient Land of Canaan appears only in the vision of Ez in 47-48. But it is characteristic that the Land of Canaan appears here in a Messianic Law Code, modelled on the ancient Priestly Code. The Land of Canaan is here an archaic ideal, bordered by the Jordan and the Gateway to Hamath. As against this, *in his prophecies* Ezekiel speaks in the

55) V. Kraetzschmar, Die Bundesvorstellung im A. T. pp. 59 sqq ; Gunkel, Comm. on Gen 15 18 ; Holzinger, Comm. on Ex 23 31 ; Gressmann, ZAW 1924, p. 336 (on Deut 11 22) ; Jeremias, Das A. T. im Lichte des alten Orients, 1916, pp. 500 sqq.

language of his own time. To *Tyre* and *Sidon* he prophesies *destruction*, but he does not prophecy that Israel will occupy their territory (27-28). He prophesies the return of Israel "to its land" (34 13 36 24), the rebuilding of the desolate cities as of old (36 4 10·11 33·55), Israelite re-occupation of the land wherein their fathers have dwelt (37 25). There is no mention here of either the Euphrates or the Jordan as borders.

The Messianic vision also contains "a patriotic dream" of an *imperialistic* nature. One element of this is the promise that Israel shall rule, either politically or religiously and morally, over other nations, or even "all the nations". This includes the vision of a king to whom the peoples shall look for guidance (Is 11 10), who shall rule "unto the ends of the earth" (Zech 9 9·10), and a vision of "aliens" who shall rebuild the walls of Jerusalem (Is 60 9·12), and so on. But this vision too has nothing to do with "the Land of Canaan".

Conversely, in the Pentateuch and in Joshua the promise of "the Land of Canaan" does not appear in any assurance of redemption from the Exile. It is not connected with the *return* to the land after Destruction and Exile. It means no more and no less than the territory intended for the *Conquerors of the Land* in the time of Moses, Joshua and Judges. It is a conception which belongs to an early, not a late period. Here we have a complement of the fact that "the Land of Canaan" does not occur in the Messianic vision.

There is also no connection between "the Land of Canaan" and the empire of David and Solomon. In the first place, "the Land of Canaan", as has already been said, is conceived not as an empire, but solely as the territory of an ethnic community. It was nowhere promised that an Israelite king would rule over this territory, or that its peoples would serve Israel. The Israelites were given this land to live in, after they should have driven out the previous inhabitants. Again, the country's borders are completely at variance with those of the Israelite Empire. It does not even include *Transjordania!* This contradiction alone proves that "the Land of Canaan" has nothing to do with the Israelite Empire. Hence the term must have been coined *before* the Conquest of *Transjordania*.

THE DATE OF JOSHUA'S LAND

From what has been said it is likewise clear that *the Land of Israel in Josh* does not pre-suppose the "grossisraelitische Idee" of David's kingdom (Mowinckel). On the contrary, the book of Joshua contains no mention at all of the Kingdom. In it the Land of Israel, so far from being envisaged as the centre of imperial rule, is a territory given as an inheritance to a confederation of *tribes* which have no king. The Kingdom is not mentioned here even as promise for the *future*! Moreover, its borders are not those of David's kingdom (v. supra, p. 54). The Land of Israel in Josh is not the handiwork of late scribes who cut up "documents" of various date and collected fragments of information from various books and then, by pasting, editing and adding, produced from all this an assorted patchwork of a "map". Nor does it owe its existence to late ethnographic "research" drawn from a "popular tradition" about tribal boundaries which had been effaced hundreds of years before. No. The Land of Joshua is a conception *peculiar to its own time*. We do not find it in the Pentateuch, and by the time of the Judges it is already out-of-date. On the map of Joshua's Land has been marked an ethnographic process which began with the Conquest of Transjordania and ended with Dan's migration to the north. There is not a single line on it later than this. It is a composite, many coloured, dynamic map. It contains "theoretical" and "utopian" areas. On it the process of occupation at the beginning of the Conquest and distribution of the Land is noted with precision. On it the ideal and utopian Land of Canaan is overlaid by the area of actual conquest, the gaps in the tribal occupations are noted and also the great national gap — up to the Gateway to Hamath; with, on the other hand, the external addition of Transjordania. To this map has been added Joshua's national legacy: his instruction to complete the Conquest. These features fix its date: *after* the deviation from the original ideal as told in Nu 21 and *before* the coming into being of the static Land of Israel "from Dan to Beersheba".

THE PROBLEM OF THE COMPLETE CONQUEST.

The history of the impulse to occupy the Land of Canaan, its appearance as an ancient divine promise, its collision with reality at the time of the Conquest of Transjordania, its partial fulfilment under Joshua, the appearance of the problem of the complete conquest and the closing of this problem — all these constitute an instructive chapter which is of the utmost importance in assessing the literature dealing with the Conquest. Joshua's Land includes a *utopian aspiration*: Joshua's legacy to the nation that it should complete the conquest of the Land of Canaan. An examination of the Biblical literature shows us, however, that Joshua's national legacy presents a live problem *only* in Josh 1 — Ju 3. The books after Ju do not deal with this problem at all. That is to say, after the period of Judges the problem was forgotten and became simply a literary and archaeological question. The correct understanding of this development is decisive in fixing the date of Josh and Ju.

From Gen 15 to Josh 1 we several times find the promise that the Israelites shall occupy the whole of Canaan up to the Euphrates, or to the Gateway to Hamath, and drive out all its peoples: Gen 15 18 Ex 23 23 27-28 31 Nu 34 2 9 Deut 1 7-8 3 21 7 16 19 9 1-3 11 23-25 31 3-8 Josh 1 2-5. This promise is *absolute* and *unconditional*. An integral part of it is the warning to Israel to expel *all* the inhabitants of Canaan and not to make a covenant with them: Ex 23 31-33 34 14-16 Nu 33 51-56 Deut 7 1-5 16-24 20 16-17. In Ex 23 29-30 Deut 7 22 it is stated that the expulsion will not be completed "in one year", but "little by little". But neither areas of conquest nor stages of expulsion and occu-

pation are laid down here. In Nu 33 55-56 the Israelites are warned
that, if they do not expel all the inhabitants of the Land, those
that are left will become their sworn foes and expel them from
their land. In Nu 34 the Israelites are commanded to divide *all*
the Land, up to the Gateway to Hamath, among the tribes. In
Deut 31 2-8 the task of apportioning the Land among the Israelites
is assigned to *Joshua*. In Josh 1 1-6 Joshua is promised that he
himself will conquer all the Land, up to the Euphrates.

Now, in Josh 13 1-6 a new conception makes its appearance:
"the remaining country". The time is the end of Joshua's wars.
Joshua is an old man. He has smitten the Canaanite from the
Negev to Baal Gad (13 7-8), but he has not gained in "Joshua's
Land" a special region called "the remaining country", a region
which does not exist in the Land of Canaan of the Pentateuch.
In "the remaining country" a new people is settled: the later
Philistines. The task of expelling the peoples of "the remaining
country" is assigned by Joshua in his national testament to the
coming generation. "The remaining country" is actually a composite area, containing territory which *was allotted but not conquered*
(the coast up to the border of Zidon), and territory which *was
neither allotted nor conquered* (from Baal Gad to the Gateway of
Hamath). This gives rise to a certain confusion in the narrative [56].

56) This confusion is rooted in the nature of the case and there is no
point in attributing the description of "the remaining territory" in vv. 2-6
to a mistaken "supplementer", as Noth does in his Comm. p. 47. "There still
remained very much of the Land to inherit" (1) is explained by Noth as
meaning that till then they had established themselves only in the area "around
Gilgal" where the camp was, and now they had to settle in the rest of the
Land as well. Only, according to Noth, the "supplementer" erroneously thought
that the reference was to the territory which had not yet been conquered.
This interpretation is illogical. How could it be said of *all the Land*, apart
from the camp area, that "very much" of it remained? And what sense then
do the opening words make: "Thou art old, advanced in years"? The meaning
of this introduction is plain: thou art old and therefore cannot complete
the conquest, cf. Josh 23 2 14 Deut 31 2-3. But the essential point is that 13-
19 speak of the distribution of *all* the Land amongst the tribes, and not of

For all that, there is here a clear promise, absolute and unconditional, that Jahweh will drive out the inhabitants of this
region from before the Israelites (13 6).

Josh 23 contains the first mention of the conception of "the
remaining peoples" (vv. 4 7 12). Here we meet, for the first time,
the warning that, if the Israelites enter into relations with these
remaining peoples, Jahweh will no longer expel them (vv. 12-13).
At the same time, we find here also the threat of Nu 33 55-56, that
the remaining peoples will become a snare to the Israelites and
in the end the latter will perish from off the face of their land
(v. 13). In Ju 2 1-3, the warning and the threat of Josh 23 12-13
appear as a prophecy foretelling punishment for sin, because the
people has sinned in making a covenant with the inhabitants of
the Land. The completion of the Conquest has become proble-
matical: it is now conditional and may not be realized.

However, in the historiosophical framework of Ju (viz: in the
main pragmatic section, Ju 2 11 — 3 6) the hope of completing
the Conquest *is entirely abandoned.*

This section contains a review of the whole era of Judges,
an explanation of the people's history during that era and a

the distribution of "remaining" territory. These chapters assume that, before
the allocation of portions, there was no settlement anywhere, not even "around
Gilgal", seeing that the settlement was by tribes. Hence, if, *before* the distribution, the phrase "remaining territory" is used, it can only mean the
territory which remained unconquered. — It is true that there is something
of a discrepancy between the opening words of 13 1-6 and the description of
the territorial distribution. In v. 6 it is said of "the remaining territory": "only
allot it to Israel for an inheritance", whereas in fact there remained an area
which *had never been included in the territory for distribution.* But since part of
the "remaining territory" (the coast up to Zidon) was actually included in
the allocation, the author allowed himself an exaggeration. It should be noted
that the phrase הפלה... בנחלה is reminiscent of Nu 34 2, and Josh 13 7-8 harks
back to Nu 34 13-15. Nu 34, however, speaks of the distribution of *all* the
Land, up to the Gateway to Hamath. The Pentateuch does not know of any
partial allocation of Canaan! It is this discrepancy between the ideal and the
real that the author covers up in v. 6. Similarly, Josh 23 4.

valuation of its results. The commentators have wrapped this
section in a thick veil of "excisions" and "amendments", thereby
completely distorting its meaning. True, the narrative is here
somewhat confused and obscure. But this does not justify the
"excisions" and "amendments". To understand the section, we
must first of all rid ourselves of the erroneous view that the
surrounding nations referred to in it are the remnants of the
Canaanites who are mentioned in Ju 1. These few remnants do
not appear in the narratives of the period of Judges as a religious or political factor of any importance. The pragmatic
section speaks not of isolated enclaves, but of "the *peoples* round
about them" (v. 12), also "their enemies round about" (v. 14), who
have enslaved Israel. This meaning is clearly vouched for by the
parallel passage which continues our pragmatic section, Ju 10 6-16.
Hence Ju 3 3 is not a later addition, but belongs to the original
text and explains the true purpose of the passage 2 20 — 3 4. Our
pragmatic section is the continuation of Josh 13 and 23, and of
Ju 2 1-3 [57]. It too deals with the question of Joshua's national

---

57) Rudolph, Elohist, pp. 263 sqq., regards Ju 1 1 — 2 5 as the introduction
to the Book of Judges. The purpose of this introduction is made clear in 2 1-5 :
to indict Israel with sin. C. 1 is meant merely to provide the material for
this indictment: the Israelites did not expel all the Canaanites and even let
one man and his family go free from the city of Luz. But c. 1 does not
in fact contain *any substance of an indictment*, nor is there any indication in
it of such an intention. According to 2 3 the sin consisted in making a covenant with the Canaanites and failing to throw down their altars. C. 1, on
the other hand, mentions only the *expulsion* of the Canaanites or their *enforced
vassalage*, and says nothing about the making of a covenant with them. There
is no mention at all of their altars. It is inconceivable that letting one man
go from Luz was regarded by this "Deuteronomistic scribe" as a national sin
and an example of covenant-making. Moreover, in 2 3 the author speaks only
of *expelling* the Canaanites (cf. Ex 23 28-3 , et al.) and not of *putting them to
the ban*. Hence it was permissible to let even all the Canaanites go. That
2 1-5 does not refer to c. 1 can be seen from the threat that "the inhabitants
of the Land" will be thorns in the side of Israel (2 3), while, in the stories
about the period of Judges, the Canaanite communities which were listed in

testament concerning the completion of the Conquest. Its attitude is most instructive.

In Ju 2 21 — 3 4 we are told why Joshua did not fully accomplish the charge assigned to him and did not expel all the inhabitants of the Land of Canaan: the nations listed in 3 3 (from Josh 13 2-6) had been allowed to remain by Jahweh and had not been given into Joshua's hand in order to test by them whether Israel would keep "the way of Jahweh" or not. The Israelites did not withstand the test. They did not observe Joshua's dying instructions (Josh 23) not to intermarry with the remaining peoples and not to worship their gods, but did intermarry and worship those gods, the Baalim and the Ashtaroth (Ju 3 5-6). They were also influenced by other neighbouring peoples (ibid 10 6-16). For this reason God gave them into the power of spoilers and into the power of their enemies round about (ibid. 2 11-15). In their affliction the Israelites cried to Jahweh and he raised up delivering Judges (v. 17). But the repentance and the deliverance were only temporary. The Judges could not root out idolatry from Israel. On the contrary, each generation was more corrupt than the last: "when the Judge died, they turned back and dealt more corruptly than their fathers" etc. (17-19). The whole era was therefore one of calamity and enslavement. But, on account of the ever-increasing corruption, there was pronounced upon Israel, apart from the transient penalties, a *permanent* doom: Jahweh decreed that He would no longer expel any "of the nations whom Joshua left when he died" (20-21). The *threat* in Josh 23 13 becomes in Ju 2 20-21 a *final sentence*. In other words, the sinfulness of the period of Judges completely annulled the promise to expel "the remaining peoples" and to complete the Conquest. "The remaining country" was subtracted from the inheritance of Israel as defined in the ancient promise. This marked *the withdrawal of the hope for the complete conquest of the Land of Canaan.*

---

c. 1 pass almost unmentioned. 2 1-5 is to be understood in the light of 2 11 — 3 6 6 7-8 10 6-16: the reference is to the whole peoples who remained in Greater Canaan and not to the fractions listed in c. 1. — On Rudolph's analysis of Ju 1 v. infra, note 66.

Thus we find a clear line of development from Gen 15 to Ju 3. We see how the ancient aspiration to occupy the Land of Canaan swerves through its collision with reality at the end of Moses' life; how it is refracted in the time of Joshua; how it is mutilated in the period of the Judges; and how the hope of its complete realization is finally abandoned at the end of that period. Each stage is reflected in a corresponding stratum of the ancient Biblical literature. Each stage has a corresponding and different "map" of the Land of Canaan and of Israel.

The Higher Criticism has sought by all the means in its power to obscure this monumental evidence. It has everywhere discovered the finger marks of editors, inserters, supplementers and later hands, "later patriots", and so on and so forth, who, from ulterior motives and through misunderstanding the text etc., made it into a confused patchwork. Against all this stands the clear evidence of the no less monumental fact that the problem of the complete conquest of Canaan was a *forgotten problem* in later generations. It was considered *for the last time* in Ju 2-3, and thenceforth *the question disappeared for ever*! Neither David nor Solomon, nor anyone after them, aspires to carry out Joshua's national testament. No prophet, no patriot, no dreamer of dreams demands the "completion" of the Conquest. Neither the promise in Josh 13 6, nor the threat in Josh 23 13 and in Ju 2 3, nor the final decree in Ju 2 20-21, is subsequently referred to or mentioned anywhere. Still more astonishing is the apparent disappearance from the popular consciousness of the very fact that the Conquest was not complete. Between Josh 13 and 23, on the one hand, and Ju 2 on the other, comes Josh 24, in which it is said that Jahweh *drove out* all the peoples of Canaan from before Israel (vv. 12-18). The whole Biblical literature after Ju 3 follows the assumption that Jahweh drove out or destroyed the Canaanites from before the Israelites and there is no reference to the incompleteness of the process. "I destroyed the Amorite from before you", says Amos (2 9). One says "from Dan to Beersheba", but one also takes the licence of saying "from the Gateway to Hamath to the Wadi of Egypt" (1 Ki 5 5   8 65). Even in Josh the tendency to an overdrawn, fictitious summing up of the occupation is recognizable (v. apart from 24 12 18, also 13 7 21 41-43 23 14). After Ju 3 the incompleteness of the Conquest is mentioned only once, in a historical psalm recalling the sins of Israel in ancient times (Ps 106 34). This sin is not mentioned in any other rebuke in the Bible. It is thus clear that the promise about the taking of all Canaan and the ancient and forgotten problem of the completion of the Conquest have their life-root in the events *of the period of the Conquest.* From then onwards they were preserved only in the ancient literature.

THE ANTIQUITY OF THE PRAGMATIC FRAMEWORK OF JU

It follows, then, that the pragmatic framework of Ju is concerned in Ju 2-3 with a special problem which was unknown to later generations. The view that this framework is "Deuteronomistic", a product of the 7th Century or later, cannot be correct. In the 7th Century there was no question of completing the Conquest. It is true that the framework is Deuteronomistic in style, but this style is ancient. We have already remarked that the historical records prior to 1 Ki 3 contain no mention of the idea of unification of the cult in the sense of the Josianic D. The evaluation of the period of Judges in Ju 2-3 is wholly unfavourable. It was a period of ever-increasing corruptness. The generations of that era were punished for their sinfulness. And for the sinfulness of the whole era a permanent doom was pronounced upon the nation. By the time of the author there was no longer any hope or ambition to complete the Conquest. But the problem still exercised the minds of the historiographers. The author found an explanation for the annulment of the ancient promise in the corruptness of the period of Judges. Even in the collection of stories there is a striking tendency to portray the period between Joshua and Saul in an unfavourable light. Gideon sets up an Ephod, thereby bringing sin on Israel; the kingdom of Abimelech goes down in blood-stained sin; Jephthah sacrifices his daughter; the time of Eli and his sons is one of sinfulness; and the period closes with military disaster and the capture of the Ark. Cc. 17-21 describe deeds of dreadful violence. The refrain is: "In those days there was no king and each man did what was right in his own eyes". The background of the Book of Judges, including its historiosophical evaluation of the era, is undoubtedly *the idealization of the Kingdom*. It was written at the beginning of the Kingdom, in the glorious days of David or Solomon. It is the Kingdom that brings deliverance from the afflictions which beset Israel in the time of the Judges (v. 2 Sam 7 10-11). And because this historiographer was close to the period of Judges, the problem of the completion of the Conquest was still very much alive for him. The hope itself he gives up.

The antiquity of the historiosophy of Ju proves that the narrative material is extremely ancient. This historian used material which belongs to the period of Judges and is not the result of later "redaction". The view, that neither narratives nor historical material from the period of the Conquest and the wars of the Judges have come down to us, is just another of the prejudices of the Higher Criticism.

THE CHARACTER OF THE NARRATIVES: LOCAL STORIES
AND AETIOLOGICAL LEGENDS

It is a current view that the stories in Josh 2-11 and in Ju
were shaped as *national* stories only at a later date. In their
original form (it is argued) they were tribal and local, *separate*
stories which did not constitute a single work, and which were
united into a national whole only by the "theocratic" redaction.
Wellhausen and his school sought to prove that the Judges were
in fact merely local, tribal heroes, whose field of action was
their tribe or their clan, and who were in no way national,
"theocratic" rulers governing Israel in a continuous line from
generation to generation. The local and tribal version of the
stories can still be extracted from the theocratic-national redaction. The assumption is that at that period Israel was not
yet one people. There were only tribes. — The stories in Joshua
had already been interpreted by Gressmann as a redaction of
separate, local *aetiological* legends. This view was developed
especially by Alt and Noth and their followers. These stories
as they appear in their late redaction relate the national war of
all the tribes of Israel, the conquerors of the Land of Canaan.
But in reality the stories are independent of one another, they
live their own life, each one having been woven on its own local
aetiological warp. Their topographical setting is very limited:
the events take place mainly in the territory of *Benjamin*. Hence
these stories originate in the tribal tradition of Benjamin, and
the shrine at *Gilgal* is their birthplace. They were originally
intended to explain the following matters: the sanctity of Gilgal
(Josh 5 13-15); the significance of its twelve stones (3-4); its
"Hill of Foreskins" (5 2-9); the ruins of Jericho (6); the mound

of Ai (8 1-29) ; the pile of stones in Emeq Achor (7) ; the existence of the family of Rahab in Israel (2 6 22-25) ; the agreement with the Gibeonites (9) ; the five trees in front of the cave of Maqqedah which was blocked with stones (10 16-27). These stories, now generalized and nationalized, were artificially brought into a single collection and set in the framework of a national plan of conquest which they do not fit.

BETWEEN JOSH AND JU
THE EVIDENCE OF THE SONG OF DEBORAH

Between the stories in Josh and those in Ju there is the fundamental difference, that in the latter the local and tribal element stands out and is easily recognizable. The tribes are settled each in its own territory. The tribal descent of the Judges is explicitly related and the beginning of their activities takes place in the territory of their tribe and its immediate neighbourhood. The local and tribal background is recognizable in the stories about Ehud, Barak and Deborah, Gideon, Abimelech, Jephthah, Samson, as also in the brief reports on the other Judges. It is otherwise with the stories in Josh. Here we have to do with *an army* in camp. The tribes have not yet occupied their portions. The events occur in certain places, each place being in the *future* portion of a certain tribe. But, *at the time of the events*, not Israelite tribes, but *Canaanites*, are in occupation of these places. Josh separates the *wars* of Canaan from the *territorial occupation* by the tribes, the time of the *conquest* from the time of the *apportionment*. The people does not obtain land property in the places where it conquers the Canaanites. The people lives in a military camp. The allocation of territory is by lot and begins at the end of the great wars. The wars are fought in the Land of Canaan and not in the Land of Israel. For this reason, while the recovery of the tribal background to the stories in Ju has something to base itself on in the text, this is not the case in Josh. Here the attempt to find a tribal stratum is not supported by textual analysis, but simply postulated by dogma. The tribal element is artificially inserted into the text by scholars, who have recourse to fanciful inventions in the manner of the Midrash exegesis by "allusion".

Here analysis is not sufficient for their purposes. A "re-creation" is required, an imaginative reconstruction of the whole book.

Even with regard to the stories in Ju, however, it should be stressed that the local and tribal element in them does not justify the conclusion that the stories were not *national* from the moment of their creation. History knows of many local events which became the occasion for national events, and of many local heroes who became national heroes. The Judges were not "theocratic" rulers in Wellhausen's sense. But there were amongst them men who became the leaders of a tribal confederation. The assumption that at that period Israel did not yet exist as a nation is fundamentally mistaken, as we see from the Song of Deborah (Ju 5). There is general agreement that this Song has come down to us in its original form, without any "theocratic" redaction. Wellhausen stresses its local and tribal character, as against the "theocratic" prose narrative (Ju 4). He maintains that, in the Song, Deborah does not "judge Israel" (4 4), but is the seer of her tribe — Issachar (5 15). Barak does not fight at the command of the national prophetess, but for personal vengeance (5 12, reading ‏ושבה שֶׁבְיָךְ‎). But what are the actual facts? The Song does describe the war as a *national* war. It is the war of "Israel", "the people of Jahweh" and the Song is sung to "the God of Israel". It recalls "the days" of Shamgar and Jael and describes the condition "of Israel" in those days. Deborah herself is "a mother in Israel". She lauds the tribes who went out to war and pours scorn on those who held back. The war is even described against a cosmic background: Jahweh appeared from Edom, the earth quaked, the skies dropped, the stars fought in their courses. The war is in fact Jahweh's war; the people merely comes "to the aid of Jahweh" in his fight against *his foes*. — The question of the number of the tribes which at that time constituted "Israel" has no decisive bearing upon our discussion. The view that Judah was then still outside "Israel" is one of the most superficial of the Higher Criticism's assumptions. But that is not important for our purpose. The Song of Deborah proves beyond any doubt that, in the time of the Judges, even before the war of Sisera, *Israel* existed as a religio-national entity, a supra-tribal subject of history, action, creation. Even if the Song of Deborah is rooted in the tribe, it is still essentially a *national* creation. In it the tribal and national elements are fused into a single entity. Therefore we should reject as absurd the view that the *prose* literature of the tribes was in that period solely tribal, without any national horizon.

BENJAMIN AND GILGAL

Still less is there any sense in the attempt at a tribal "re-creation" of Josh.

Even if it were possible to prove that the stories in Josh were of *Benjamite* provenance, that would not mean that their original character was "Benjamite" rather than Israelite and national. The story-tellers and bards of Benjamin were no less nationally conscious than those of Naphtali, Zebulun and Issachar. They could have related the history of Israel's wars from the standpoint of their own tribe. But, in fact, the whole Benjamite theory is a figment of the imagination. In all the stories of Josh there is not *one single mention* of Benjamin. The tribe is not even mentioned in the story about the Gibeonites (9). It does not play any part even as *one* tribe amongst others. It is the "Children of Israel", not the Children of Benjamin, who come to the cities of the Gibeonites (9 17). The Benjamites do not appear even to request a provisional portion, and that although the war is being waged in their future territory. Indeed, *no tribe at all* plays any part in these stories. *Joshua* is one of the Children of Joseph. But we know this from another source and not from the stories. They do not mention Joshua's tribal descent, in the manner of the stories about the Judges. *The tribes of Joseph* are *not once* mentioned in the war stories. The only tribe to receive mention here is *Judah*, and even that not in a military narrative, but in the story about Achan (7).

An artificial means of producing an "allusion" to Benjamin is to locate the stories at Gilgal, in the portion of Benjamin, thus supposedly making them part of the lore of the shrine at

Gilgal. But this too is pure fancy. *The shrine* at Gilgal is *not once* mentioned or alluded to in Josh. Joshua builds an altar on Mount Ebal (8 30-35). But no altar is built at Gilgal and no cultic ceremony is performed there. Gilgal is the site of the camp where various events consequently occur, but the place is not described as the location of a cult. In Gilgal Joshua sets up the twelve stones (4 20). But these are memorial stones (ibid. 21-24). Joshua does not set up an altar on the site, nor inaugurate a festival, nor does he imply that here will be "a House of God". In Gilgal Joshua circumcises the Israelites (5 2-9). But the ceremony of the circumcision is not connected with a shrine. The operation is performed in Gilgal, because the camp was there. According to 5 10-12, the Israelites celebrated the Passover that year in Gilgal. But this too was because the camp was there. This fragment is in the style of P, and according to P the only shrine of Israel at that time was the Tent. Thus, not even in the cultic stories is there any allusion to the shrine of Gilgal, let alone in the others where Gilgal is mentioned only as a military camp. There is no truth in the view that the passage about the appearance of "the Commander of Jahweh's Host" to Joshua (5 13-15) is an explanation of the sanctity of Gilgal (Alt). The theophany occurs not in Gilgal but in Jericho and the passage is part of the story of Jericho: the appearance of the Commander of the Host announces the coming of the first great victory. Nor is it true that the legend explains the *cultic* sanctity of a shrine in Jericho (Noth). Jericho is still Canaanite and as such possesses no sanctity. The legend is not cultic, but *prophetic*. The Commander of the Host appeared there at the very moment ("just now have I come") of the Israelites' coming. The place is "holy" only by virtue of the appearance of the Commander of the Host. This is prophetic, non-cultic, sanctity, like that of the Burning Bush (Ex 3 1-5). In both these passages the removal of sandals is mentioned, but there is neither altar nor sacrifice [58]. Again, there

---

58) On the various views expressed about Josh 5 13-15 v. Rudolph, Elohist, pp. 181-182. Rudolph himself accepts the most absurd view of all — Schulz's conjecture that the original continuation of vv. 13-15 was vv. 2 sqq: the Cap-

is no truth in the view that the Gibeonites were connected with the shrine of Gilgal. There is absolutely no allusion to such a thing. — The whole "Gilgal" theory is a fantasy.

tain of the Host appeared in order to command Joshua to circumcize the Israelites on their reaching the Holy Land. "The place upon which thou art standing is holy" refers to all the Holy Land. For the sake of this interpretation Rudolph indulges in a minor orgy of critical analysis of the kind so well known, with a view to making the text fit this fantastic conjecture. For where in the Pentateuch is there any indication that the commandment of circumcision was dependent upon the Land? Furthermore, Rudolph is driven to give a false translation of v. 15: המקום is rendered by him "der Boden" (the soil, land), instead of "der Ort" or "die Stätte". In fact, the central point of the story is not in v. 15, but in v. 14 in the words "now have I come": this announces the future participation of the Commander of Jahweh's Host in the battle ranks of Israel. 5 15 emphasizes only the prophetic sanctity of the place, not the purpose of the theophany. There is thus here no "ridiculus mus" (Rudolph, ibid.), as if the Commander of the Host revealed himself only to make Joshua take off his sandals.

THE LOCATION OF THE WARS

It is true that the events related in 5-9 take place in that "corridor" between Judah and Ephraim which was to fall to the lot of Benjamin and Dan. But was not this topographical setting of the stories the natural one to choose for anyone who set about shaping the traditions and legends of the Conquest? The fact is that the Benjamite topographical background to the war stories is only part of the total setting. The events which occur in the portion of Benjamin are only a link in the chain of events which begin and end outside that portion and which pass through it from objective necessity.

The War of Conquest begins with *the crossing of the Jordan.* The camp is at Shittim (2 1) on the plains of Moab, in the portion of Gad. Therefore the natural crossing-point for the tribes is close to Jericho. Their entry into the "corridor" is thus governed by a non-Benjamite topographical factor. The actual operation of crossing the Jordan is carried out not in the portion of Benjamin, but between Gad and Benjamin. The Jordan parts for the tribes when they are in the portion of Gad. The miracle occurs along the whole line of the Jordan, not merely on the border of Benjamin. What follows from now until the capture of Debir (10 38) is a chain of military events the first links of which naturally pass through the portion of Benjamin. Indeed, it is not even entirely true that the first events occur only on the border of Benjamin. Gilgal and Emeq Achor are border-points of Judah and Benjamin (15 7 18 17) [59]; Jericho, Ai, Bethel, Beth-horon

59) Some scholars hold that הגלגל in 15 7 is corrupt and should be read

are border-points of Ephraim and Benjamin (16 1-3 18 12-14; on Ai-Aija v. Ezr 2 28 Neh 11 31 1 Chr 7 28). Gibeon too is close to the border of Ephraim. Kiriath-jearim, one of the Gibeonite cities, is on the border of Judah and Benjamin (15 9 18 14-15). The war advances by stages along the line Jericho-Ai-Gibeon-Beth-horon-Emeq Ayalon, and thence to the Shephelah. In other words, it is fought on the borders of Ephraim, Benjamin and Dan, passing from there to the border of Judah. Wright has shown that the progress of the war as described in Josh 10, from Gibeon to Debir, has an inner strategic logic [60]. But the "logic" really begins as early as Shittim. The route of the conquest is drawn by objective military factors. All this has no connection with Benjamin and the shrine at Gilgal.

If we have more detailed stories about the first events, from Shittim to Gibeon, this is simply because the author's plan was to cover the conquest of "the bridgehead" exhaustively, up to the decisive turning-point of the surrender of Gibeon, and to describe the other two great military advances only in outline.

גלילות, as in 18 17. According to 4 19 Gilgal was "at the eastern end of Jericho". In that case, Gilgal was on the *Ephraim*-Benjamin border. Gilgal is not numbered among the cities of Benjamin.

60) Wright, Problem, pp. 109—112.

THE NATIONAL CHARACTER OF THE STORIES

The fundamental difference between the stories in Josh and those in Ju undoubtedly preserves evidence of historical value. The accepted assumption is that both alike were subjected to a theocratic, national redaction. In that case, why has the tribal element completely disappeared from the stories in Josh and from them alone? It is clear that the "national" redaction had no need to *expunge* the tribal element. Joshua could just as well have been depicted as a "theocratic" commander of *tribes* fighting on separate fronts. In Josh 14 6-15 17 14-18 Joshua does actually appear in this role — at the end of the great battles. In Ju 1 1-26, the separate wars of the tribes are set in a theocratic-national framework. The only possible meaning of all this is that the national character of the stories in Josh 1-11 is *original* and that the difference between them and the stories in Ju reflects *historical reality*.

CRITICISM OF THE AETIOLOGICAL INTERPRETATION

In the stories in Josh there is a legendary element which, in its turn, contains an aetiological element. A clear aetiological motive is found in the two stories about Gilgal: 4 2-24 5 2-9. In 5 9 the explanation of the name is even explicitly stressed. The mention of the Hill of Foreskins in 5 3 is also aetiological. The explanation of a name (Emeq Achor) is similarly stressed in 7 26. It is possible that in other stories too aetiological motives are included. But does this justify the attempt to interpret this whole series of stories as "aetiological legends"? An aetiological motive may just as well be an embellishment, an inessential and incidental adornment. Only those legends can be considered truly aetiological which *owe their existence* to the aetiological motive. Is it possible to include the stories of Josh in this class?

There is a total disproportion between the stories in Josh and the aetiological motives or problems which Alt and his followers find in them. The phenomena which receive supposedly aetiological explanation are for the most part common, simple and ordinary phenomena with nothing extraordinary about them; and assuredly nobody felt any need to "explain" them.

In Emeq Achor there was *a cairn of stones* and the story about Achan is supposedly meant to explain this cairn. But did a cairn in this land of stones require any "explanation"? Could a cairn have given rise to such a story about an unprecedented ban and the brutal slaughter of an entire family? There was also a cairn before Ai (8 29); and there we find a different story. There was a cairn on Absalom's grave and in the Valley of the King was a pillar in his memory (2 Sa 18 17-18). By the method of Alt and Noth it would be possible to regard the stories about Absalom as aetiological legends about the cairn and the pillar. A legend may entwine itself about a cairn or a place and, finding there a material point d'appui, may include them as a secondary motive, but it cannot *come into being* through them.

The story about the crossing of the Jordan is supposed to be an aetiological legend explaining *the twelve stones* at Gilgal. But, after all, cromlech stones were found everywhere and had nothing phenomenal about them. How could it have occured to anyone "to explain" these stones by inventing such a unique legend as the parting of the Jordan? In the shrine of Bethel there were the pillar and the altar of Jacob (Gen 28 11-22 35 1-7 9-15). In Mizpah there were a cairn and a pillar set up by Jacob (ibid. 31 44-52). In the shrine of Shechem there was a "great stone" set up by Joshua (Josh 24 26-27). In Ophrah stood Gideon's altar of Jahweh (Ju 6 24), and an altar of Baal destroyed by Gideon (ibid. 25-34). In Ophrah there was also a stone on which Abimelech slew his brothers (ibid. 9 5 18). Beside a ruined tower in Tebez there lay, apparently, the millstone by which Abimelech was killed (ibid. 53 2 Sam 11 21). In the field of Joshua at Beth-shemesh there was "a large stone" on which the Ark was placed (1 Sam 6 18). Between Mizpah and the Crag stood Samuel's "Stone of Help" (ibid. 7 12). Somewhere between Mizpah and Ayalon there was "a large stone" which Saul made into an altar (ibid. 14 31-35). There were several other such altars of Saul in the Land (ibid. 35). On the threshing-floor of *Araunah* stood an altar set up by David (2 Sam 24 21-25). On Mount Carmel there was an altar of twelve stones built by Elijah (1 Ki 18 30-38). By the method of Alt and Noth we ought to interpret all that is related about Jacob, Joshua, Gideon, Abimelech, Saul, etc., in these stories as aetiological legends about the stones and the altars. But how could these stones and altars, which were similar to those found everywhere in the Land, have been the source of inspiration for all these stories? Of the pillar of Jacob at Bethel we are explicitly told that it was simply an ordinary stone, "one of the stones of the place" (Gen 28 11 18).

It is likewise incredible that the story about the killing of the five kings, their being hung on trees and their being cast into the cave at *Maqqedah* (Josh 10 16-27) should have been invented to explain the cave blocked with stones at Maqqedah and the five trees in front of it. After all, caves too, open or closed, with or without trees, are found everywhere in this land. They are just the sort of places in which legends inhere, but they are not extraordinary phenomena such as could give rise to legends. How could a cave with trees in front of it have brought into being the grim legend about the hanging of men slain in battle — an act without parallel in the Bible outside Josh? In the story about Gideon's war with Midian caves and shafts, in which the Israelites hid, are mentioned (Ju 6 2). Caves are also mentioned in the story of Saul's battle against the Philistines at Michmash (1 Sam 13 6 14 11). Caves play a certain part in the stories about David and Saul (ibid. 22 1 24 4-23 2 Sam 23 13). Obadiah hides a hundred prophets in caves (1 Ki 18 4 13). Elijah spends the night in a cave on Mount Horeb (ibid. 19 9-18). Are we to say that these are all aetiological legends about the caves? In the story about Ai there is no cave. But here a single tree and a cairn of stones gave rise to a legend about the hanging of a slain king (Josh 8 29). But how could ordinary trees beside a cave or cairns have prompted the conception of the hanging of men killed in battle? There were trees everywhere and on each one of them somebody could have been hung. Nor does the text state that there was only *one tree* at Ai, or that there were only *five trees* at Maqqedah. Only the *hanging* trees are mentioned, but the total number of trees in the place is not stated. The fixing of the total number is an invention of Alt and Noth. The trees in front of the Cave of Machpelah (Gen 23 17) did not give rise to any legends about hanging. — Trees appear in the Bible in several legends and stories. They appear in the legends about Abraham (Gen 18 1-4 21 33) and Gideon (Ju 6 11). In the story in Josh 24 the oak in the sanctuary at Shechem is mentioned (v. 26). Deborah sits beneath a palm (Ju 4 5). Saul sits under a pomegranate tree (1 Sam 14 2) or under a tamarisk (ibid. 22 6). But it is obvious that all these are not aetiological tree legends.

Again, the story about Rahab cannot be taken as an aetiological legend. Supposing that there was such a Canaanite family in Israel, was it the *only one* and was there about its existence anything phenomenal requiring a legendary explanation? Was there an aetiological legend about *every* Canaanite family? Noth arbitrarily retouches the Rahab story to make the suggestion plausible. Thus, the family of Rahab dwelt for generations in the ruins of Jericho. "The house of Rahab" still existed in the wall of Jericho. A scarlet thread was still hung in the window. The daughters of the house followed Rahab's calling. But all this is pure fantasy. It is not related that the family of Rahab remained *in Jericho*[61]. The expression "the house of Rahab" (Noth's inverted commas) does not exist in the text. Moreover, in 6 25 we are not told that the *descendants* of Rahab are dwelling in Israel "unto this day". Neither sons nor daughters of Rahab are mentioned in the story. We are told only of *Rahab herself*, that she is dwelling amongst the Israelites "unto this day". The story-teller speaks as one of the same generation writing in Rahab's lifetime and it is her presence in Israel, together with her father's household, that he explains. "Unto this day" is an extremely wide expression.

61) According to Windisch, ZAW 1917/18, p. 194; Hölscher, ZAW 1919/20, p. 55; Rudolph, Elohist, p. 169, Rahab dwelt in *Israelite* Jericho. But there is no hint of an *Isralite* Jericho in these stories. That Rahab and her female descendants were temple-prostitutes has already been argued by Hölscher, ibid. pp. 56—57. Rudolph rightly maintains against him that there is no indication of this in the text.

THE INNERMOST IDEA OF THE STORIES OF JOSH

The stories in Josh 1-11 bear a legendary stamp. Moreover, the legendary element is the *essence* of these stories, expressing as it does the idea which gives them their life and form. Anyone who splits them into fragments by artificial critical analysis and with the aid of subjective insertions turns them into local, aetiological legends has not grasped their true character. We have here six sets of narratives: the crossing of the Jordan, the conquest of Jericho, the affair of Ai and the affair of Achan, the surrender of Gibeon, the victory over the kings of the south, the victory over the kings of the north. The contents of these narratives are not "local", even in their minutest detail. The only places where any aetiological element at all appears are 5 2-9 and 7 25-26, in secondary particulars. The master-design of all these stories is a single idea: that the Conquest of the Land is a *miraculous sign*. The Israelites did not conquer the Land by their own power. The Canaanites were mighty men, their cities were fortified, they had horses and chariots. The Conquest can be understood only as the finger of God — a sign that Jahweh is "God in the heavens above and on the earth beneath" (2 11), and that the "living God" is in the midst of Israel (3 10). This idea is not "local". It is *Israelite*, Israel's original creation. The wonders in Josh are of an Israelite pattern. They are not deeds of *magic*. They *are performed only once*, at the time specially appointed for them ; they are sparks of the supreme divine will, and God proclaims beforehand where and how they will come to pass. It was not the Priests and the people who parted the waters of the Jordan or laid flat the walls of Jericho. They did *what God ordered* and at the appointed time God's word came to pass. This idea was not superimposed on the legends by a late literary redaction. It is part of their original warp; it is the fountain-head of their creation. This idea in Israel shaped the narratives of the real events even as they came into being, at the earliest stage of their oral creation, from the moment when the happenings were formed into *a story* in the mouth of those who had lived through them. There never was a "realistic" account of the events. The account of the events was "idealistic", "legendary", right from the start. Every warrior who came from the battle-line to the camp and told his story to the women and children related "legendary" things, "idealistic" history stamped with the idea of the miraculous sign. It is this Israelite idea that brought into being all the stories ever told about the Conquest of the Land, including those preserved in Josh. In Josh 1-11 there is hardly a *single letter* which does not express this idea.

The stories depict the Conquest of the Land as a two-fold miraculous sign: in the realm of the spirit and in the realm of matter. God strengthened the heart of Israel while he melted the heart of the Canaanites. Again, he increases *the power* of Israel, cleaves a way before them, and *smites* the Canaanites. The effect of the wonders is two-fold: they spread teror amongst the Canaanites and strengthen the morale of Israel, and at the same time they assist in the material victory over the Canaanites. This is the ideological background of all these stories. The Israelites fought the Canaanites in four encounters: at Jericho, at Ai, against the confederation of the southern kings, against the confederation of the northern kings. But the outcome of each encounter was decided in advance by God's words to Joshua: "Behold, I have given them into your hand..." (6 2 8 1 10 8 11 6). The battles are simply the translation into fact of God's word.

This conception of the wars of Canaan finds expression in the story about *Rahab* which serves as the introduction to them. The wars of Canaan are the continuation of the Exodus from Egypt and the Conquest of Transjordania. Rahab does not help the Israelites to conquer Jericho, she does not disclose secrets to them, she does not give them signals[62]. She merely expresses the terror and dismay of the Canaanites before the might of Israel's God (2 9-11 24). — *The crossing of the Jordan* is a miraculous sign, a sign of "the living God" and of his prophet (4 14). The stones of Gilgal preserve the memory of this sign for future generations (4 20-24). The crossing of the Jordan struck terror into the kings of Canaan "and they had no more spirit" (5 1). This legend is not meant to explain the significance of twelve stones. The Israelite idea transmuted the crossing of the Jordan into a miraculous sign and created this legend as its own symbol. The Jordan, the Ark, the Priests, the people, Joshua are used as material elements which the idea disposes in conformity with the symbol. It even casts its spell over the stones, turning them into a memorial to a unique miraculous sign. — The theophany of the *"Commander of the Host"* to Joshua, before the first clash with the Canaanites, also symbolizes the idea of the finger of God: Israel does not fight, but God fights for them. — So it is with the ceremony of the conquest of *Jericho*. Although the material subject of the legend is different, it bears the same stamp as the crossing of the Jordan. Here too we find a ceremony in which the great mass of the people participates and which serves as the setting for an only once performed miraculous divine sign. These are not separate legends explaining stones or ruined walls. In both one and the same idea is at work which transmutes the material in one and the same spirit.

The other stories too are shaped by this idea.

The stories in 7-8 differ from those about the Jordan and Jericho in that they describe the Israelites as performing *actual military* operations, defeating their enemies not by ceremonies, but by the sword and by battle tactics. But even these deeds are shaped by the Israelite idea into a miraculous sign.

According to the story in 7-8, the miraculous victorious pro-

---

62) This is emphasized by Rudolph, ibid., against Windisch and Hölscher (v. note 61) who state that Rahab betrayed Jericho to the Israelites by showing them the entry into the city. Windisch quotes instances from Roman literature of prostitutes who betrayed cities to the enemy.

gress is suddenly stopped. The Israelites receive a set-back before Ai and flee. The story explains both the defeat and the subsequent victory as the finger of God. The; people disregarded the ban and their God, therefore, left them. They were victorious when they earned God's pardon. In the story in 7-8 it seems possible to separate the story of Achan from the story of Ai and to extract a separate "local" story about the conquest of Ai, a local "aetiological legend" explaining the mound of Ai[63]. According to the text of the "local" story the defeat was due not to the transgression of Achan, but to *the error of the spies* who recommended sending only about three thousand men to Ai (7 2-3). The defeat made the people aware of their mistake, whereupon they all went out to battle and, by employing military tactics and setting an ambush, took the city. But this "aetiological legend" is most *realistic*, with nothing of "legend" about it. Moreover, all these details — the defeat, the rout, the ambush, the tactical flight etc. — are quite unnecessary to explain the desolate mound of Ai. On the other hand, it is clear that the narrative of Achan contained some tale about divine wrath and about a national *defeat* which brought about the severe punishment of Achan. Thus the stories about Achan and Ai naturally complete each other. The realistic arrangement of the story about Ai, as seen even in its detailed topographical descriptions, shows that here we have a tradition about a *historical* event. This has not been refuted by archaeology[64]. The realistic historical material

---

63) Noth, Josua, pp. 23-28.

64) From the excavations of Marquet-Krause at Et-tell in the years 1933, 1934/5 (v. Syria, 1935, pp. 326 —345) the aetiologists have jumped to over-hasty conclusions. Not only has the whole tel not been excavated, but it is probable that Ai was in another place than Et-tell. Weighty proofs of this probability were adduced by Grintz, העי אשר עם בית און, סיני, אב־אלול, תש"ז: pp. 219-228. Noth, Josua, p. 25, says that the whole story in Josh 7-8 shows that Ai contained a Benjamite community since the time of the Conquest, in contradiction of what is related in 8 28. For clearly, argues Noth, the name Ai means "Ruin", and unless there had been a settlement there, so called on account of its being on the tel, the name would never have been preserved. Since the excava-

was subjected to the ideological interpretation and modified by it. This interweaving of the two elements undoubtedly reflects *the actual circumstances*: the elements were interwoven *in life*. The double explanation of the defeat (the transgression and the spies' error) is in the true style of Biblical narrative, even where the story is absolutely historical (e. g. 2 Ki 12 15). The story-teller regards the error of the spies itself as the beginning of the *punishment*: this too is the finger of God. In this spirit he continues. Joshua employs realistic tactics. But these tactics themselves are—the command of God (8 2 8)! The fate of Ai is decided not by tactics, but by God's words to Joshua: "I have given the king of Ai into your hand" etc. (8 1). Joshua gives a sign to the ambush with his javelin. But this too is done by God's command (v. 18). Even the work of the javelin is a miraculous sign.

In c. 9 the successful progress of the conquest of the "bridge-head" reaches its climax: Gibeon capitulates. It was not terror of Israel that seized them, but they came because of Jahweh the God of Israel (vv. 9-10). This capitulation foreshadows the overthrow of the Canaanites. — C. 10 also relates the military exploits of Joshua. Joshua acts as an inspired commander who knows how to exploit the strong points of his own troops and the weaknesses of the enemy. In a series of battles he carries out a strategic master-plan. But, to the story-teller's mind, all these acts are simply the performance of God's words to Joshua before the encounter: "Be not afraid of them, for I have given them into your hand" (v. 8). In this encounter God actually fights "from the heavens". He hurls "hailstones" upon the Canaanites in their flight down the slope of Beth-horon (11). At Joshua's prayer, he makes the sun stand still for a whole day

---

tions showed that the new settlement on the ancient tel had been founded only in the Iron Age, it must have been Israelite. But Grintz has already proved, in his above mentioned article, p. 225, that the premise of this argument is false. Ai does not mean "Ruin", but heap, a pile or piles of stones. עי, עיה, עית, עיים are always and only names of inhabited places and never of ruins. V. Nu 21 11 33 44-45 Josh 25 29; Is 10 28 Jer 49 3. There is thus no proof that the settlement of Ai stood on the ruins of an ancient city.

(12-14). In this spirit does the story-teller transmute the account of the northern war (11).

Legends such as the crossing of the Jordan or the capture of Jericho are *through and through* embodiments of the idea of the miraculous sign. In other words, they are Israelite, not local, *through and through*. If they are "aetiological", then they are *Israelite* solutions to aetiological problems. But in fact they are similar to the legends about the theophany of the Commander of the Host, the hail from heaven, the halting of the sun. Like these, they too are attached to places, but the fountain-head of *their creation* is the Israelite idea.

UNITY OF THE REALISTIC BACKGROUND

The truth is that not only the *idealistic* redaction of the events is homogeneous and derived from a single spiritual source: there is a unity also in the *realistic* sequence of the events, as far as we can see them through the idealistic redaction. These stories are not a collection of legends and traditions from various sources which collectors, editors and supplementers have somehow or other pasted together. They recount deeds which, as a whole and in detail, do indeed sum up to a single *plan*, the spiritual utterance of a single *personality*. Nor is this all. We may assume that it was this national programme, followed by the commander, that made possible the Conquest of the Land. Those who split up these stories into molecules of legends of various kinds and from various sources have failed to grasp not only their *spiritual* unity, but even their *realistic* significance. This point will be further discussed later.

DATE OF THE STORIES

When did these stories come into being?

Decisive is the fact that amongst all the war-stories of Josh there *is not a single one* about a battle against the *Philistines*. All the wars are simply and solely *Canaanite*. We are told that Joshua fought in the Shephelah (10 40-41 11 16). But he does not come across the Philistines. Nor is this all. In 11 22 it is stated explicitly that Gaza, Gath and Ashdod are occupied by *Anakim*, but there is no mention of the Philistines. In 12 8 the Shephelah is mentioned, but the Philistines are not listed there amongst the inhabitants of Canaan. This is all the more surprising, since the five Philistines rulers are mentioned already in 13 3. Similarly, the note on Dan's migration northwards (19 47) belongs to the Philistine period. For all that, the Philistines do not appear in the book of the wars. This is the common ground between these chapters and Ju 1 where again there is still no mention of the Philistines. It cannot, then, be doubted that these stories took shape at the beginning of the period of Judges before the Philistines of the Pentapolis appeared in the Land of Canaan.

From what has been said *the absolutely archaic character* of the Book of Joshua becomes plain.

When we join thread to thread the following ancient tapestry unfolds its colours. At the time of Joshua's wars the *Philistines* of the Pentapolis were not yet in the Land of Canaan. Joshua fought only against the Canaanite peoples. In his days the Philistine cities were still occupied by Anakim. The Philistines appear only in Josh 13, in the introduction to the Book of the Distribution of the Land. However, in this chapter Israel is unconditionally promised that they will *expel* the Philistines from the Shephelah. The real history of the Philistines is beyond the horizon of the Book of Joshua. There is no hint of awareness that they are *to remain* in the Shephelah in the period of the Kingdom also, and even after Israel shall have been exiled from its land. Jericho is waste and accursed and has not yet been rebuilt. Ai is desolate. The Gibeonites are enslaved, but continue to live in their cities: they are not yet dispersed "in the whole territory of Israel" (2 Sam 21 5). "The Land of Joshua" comes historically after "the Land of Canaan" of the ancient promise and before the historical Land of Israel, and a fortiori before the Israelite Empire. On the map of this land is marked Dan's unreal portion, but not its real territory in the north. Dan's northward migration is noted, but without any demarkation of its territory. Simeon is dwelling in the midst of Judah. Its southward expansion to Mount Seir (1 Chr 4 34-43) is not marked. The Emeq is entirely *Canaanite*. Its conquest is prevented by the *iron chariots* (Josh 17 16 18) which were no longer a decisive factor by the beginning of the period of Judges. Joshua urges only the Children of Joseph to expel the Canaanites from there. What happened in the time of Deborah is beyond the ken of the Book of Joshua. Jerusalem in the War Book is an important Canaanite royal city, while in the Book of Distribution it is a city of no importance — "Jebus" — which still has no Israelite population. Bethel has not yet been captured. Gezer is Canaanite. Hebron is occupied by Anakim and is still called "Kiriath-arba". Joshua grants it to Caleb who hopes to drive the Anakim out of it. Ayalon is in Dan's fictitious portion, but it is not yet a Benjamite city. Lod, Hadid and Ono are not mentioned. All the coast is Canaanite-Philistine. True, there is an explicit promise that Israel will *conquer* it. There is as yet no allusion to the annulment of the promise and to the renouncement of Ju 2-3. But the promise is not one of *imperial rule* over the coastal region. The dynamism of "Joshua's Land" is only ethnic. It contains a faith in ethnic expansion even into Lebanon and the territory of Tyre and Sidon, up to the Gateway to Hamath. But there is no suggestion of imperial rule. The territorial occupation of Joshua's day, although incomplete, marks a *climax*, the realization of all the hopes ("it all came to pass": Josh 21 41-43). The favour of the Kingdom is beyond the book's ken. The crystallization of the actual Land of Israel and the tendency to forgo the complete conquest of Canaan are hinted at only in c. 24. The conception of the Land of Israel "from Dan to Beersheba" has not yet taken shape. In Joshua's Land there are as yet no *temples*. Bethel is still Canaanite; the House of "the Gate of Heaven" has not yet been built. On Mount Ebal only an altar is erected. In Shiloh there stands the Tent of Meeting. Only in c. 24 do we find mention of a shrine in Shechem. The Priests are not yet scattered amongst the cities nor have they yet established themselves at the temples and bamoth. The Book of Joshua preserves an ancient and fanciful programme of actually severing the Priests and Levites from the cult and settling them in separate cities and even in separate "territories". This programme belongs to a time before the establishment of the temples and bamoth in the Land. Josh contains no allusion to the decline and affliction of the period of Judges. All is optimism [65]. The people obeys Joshua, is

---

65) Josh 24 31 is not an integral part of the book, but has been tacked

faithful to Jahweh. Future prospects are brilliant: there is a firm belief that Israel will, after Joshua's death, conquer the territory which he did not have time to conquer. C. 23 contains a warning that, if Israel falls into sin, the nations remaining in the Land will become a snare to them and expel them from off their soil. Thus the danger is impending from the west and the north. The heavy attacks from the direction of Ammon, Moab, Midian, Amalek and Aram in the period of Judges are outside the book's cognizance. There is no allusion to the special military might of the Philistines. We have already remarked that the migration of Dan northwards is the latest historical event mentioned in the Book of Joshua.

We see, then, that the examination of the Book of Joshua brings us to the same conclusion as we had drawn from our study of the historical framework of Ju, viz.: the accepted view that no authentic historical tradition about the Conquest of the Land has been preserved in the Bible is wrong. In fact, we have a literary tradition which in its extant from dates back to the beginning of the period of Ju. We shall find that this conclusion is confirmed by an examination of the relation between the Book of Joshua and the first chapter of Ju.

on to it from Ju 2 7. In Ju 2 10 the verse has its continuation, whereas in Josh it has none. In the Septuagint the verse comes in Josh 24 after v. 28. This too shows that the verse is an addition.

In Ju 1 there are some passages and verses (10⁻16 20 21 27⁻29) to which we find parallels and variants in the chapters in Josh about the territorial occupation by Judah, Ephraim and Manasseh (15 13⁻19 63 16 10 17 11⁻13). This indicates that the authors of the two books used a single source which described the tribes' occupation of their territories. The overwhelming majority of Ju 1 consists of excerpts from that source. It is generally agreed that Ju 1, like Josh, does not represent a tradition from the actual period of the Conquest, but is a late summary of the ethnographic situation as it had evolved by the time of Saul or of David and Solomon. Wright, who criticizes the accepted valuation of Josh and Ju 1, stresses the miscellaneous, fragmentary character of Ju 1 and suggests that it perhaps contains allusions (in v. 18) to the conquests of David or Uzziah [66]. However, an examination

---

66) Wright, Problem, p. 104. Rudolph, Elohist, pp. 263 sqq. analyses Ju 1 in the well-known way, finding in it fragments, additions, recensions, etc., from various times. In the analysis of 1 21⁻36 he accepts the conclusions of Feller (pp. 264, 266). The story of the conquest of Bethel (vv. 22⁻26) is older than the list of the gaps in the Conquest (21 27⁻35), because in the story "the House of Joseph" still appears as a single entity, whereas in the list the House of Joseph is already split into its component tribes. However, that this dismemberment is not valid is proved by v. 35 where the House of Joseph again appears! We further find "the House of Joseph" even in 2 Sam 19 21 Am 5 6 6 6 Ob 18. The remarks about making the Canaanites tributary in vv. 28 30 33 35, and also v. 21ᵇ are considered by Rudolph (after Feller)

of the background of this chapter shows that it is ancient from beginning to end.

Ju 1 resembles Josh 1—12 in that it is still unaware of the *Philistines*. The area of the battles described in Ju 1 1-26 stretches from Bethel to Hormah. Yet throughout this region there are only *Canaanite* settlements (1 9). The Children of Judah fight also in the Shephelah (9), and capture Gaza, Askalon and Ekron (18). But these are all wars against the Canaanite. The Danites are hard pressed by the *Amorites* (34-36), not by the Philistines as in the Samson-stories. — *Dan* is still settled in the south-west and has not yet moved northwards. — *Simeon* still has a lot of his own and Judah goes to help him in a war against the Canaanite in his lot and in the taking of Zephath-Hormah (3 17). Whereas by Saul's time Simeon's lot had already been absorbed into Judah's (1 Sam 30 26-30) ; and in the list of portions Simeon's lot appears as part of the portion of Judah (Josh 19 1-9). — In the Canaanite wars *iron chariots* feature as a decisive factor (Ju 1 19; as complement to 27-28, v. Josh 17 16 18). By the time of Sisera's war the iron chariot has no longer such im-

as additions from Saul's time. This is refuted by v. 35 where the *House of Joseph* make the Amorites tributary. The enforced vassalage of the Canaanites thus belongs to *the war of the tribes* against the Canaanites. For, by the time of the Kingdom there is no more fighting by separate tribes. Moreover, it is nowhere mentioned that Saul or David made vassals of Canaanites, and did so specifically because they could not expel them. Saul does not fight at all against the Canaanites within his borders (v. the summary in 1 Sam 14 46-48) ; and David fights only against the Jebusites in Jerusalem. In note 6 to p. 266 Rudolph asserts (against Auerbach) that in 1 Sam 31 7 (from the time of Saul) the political situation is already depicted as in Ju 1 28. But this too is incorrect. In Ju 1 28 the Emeq is *entirely Canaanite*, though it is tributary. Whereas in 1 Sam 31 7 the Emeq is *entirely Israelite* and there is no mention at all of Canaanites throughout the story there. Canaanites have been arbitrarily introduced by the critics at that point, as in many other places. In the whole of Ju 1 there is no reference to the events of the period of the Kingdom (v. infra). That from Ju 1 27 onwards only the events of the period of the Conquest are dealt with is also proved by Josh 17 12-18, as we have seen above, pp. 38-40.

portance (v. Ju 4 3 13 15 5 28). — *Gezer* is Canaanite. *The Emeq* is entirely Canaanite. *Jerusalem* is occupied by the Jebusite (in v. 21 "with the Children of Benjamin" means *in the portion* of the Children of Benjamin). "And it came to pass that Israel grew strong" (28) does *not* allude to *the Kingdom*, but to the increasing strength of *the tribes*. In v. 35 it is explicitly stated: "and the hand of the *House of Joseph* prevailed". The tribes are still fighting for themselves, as throughout the whole chapter. Whereas with the establishment of the Kingdom, the tribal war came to an end. The Canaanite cities are *autonomous*, though by agreement between them and the tribes the Canaanites are obliged to render tributary labour. — Since Dan has not yet moved northwards, it follows that the chapter is older than the Song of Deborah (v. Ju 5 17) [67]. And since the pressure upon Dan is not yet from the Philistines, it follows that the chapter is older even than the Samson-stories. — In short, Ju 1 is an ancient document, belonging to the early part of the period of Judges.

It is widely held that the heading of Ju 1, "and it came to pass after the death of Joshua", is a mistake of the editor's. On this view, the story in Ju 1 cannot be a continuation of Josh, since, according to the Book of Joshua, Joshua conquered the whole Land and distributed it, empty of inhabitants, amongst the tribes, whereas here the war is in full swing. For this reason Ju 1 should be regarded as a parallel, though entirely different, story about the Conquest of the Land to that in Josh. According to Josh, the Land of Canaan is conquered by *all the tribes together as an organized national army*. Ju 1, on the contrary, relates that the tribes conquered the Land *in separate wars*, each in its own portion. Since the tribes are not united in the period of Judges it follows that the story in Ju 1 is closer to historical truth.

---

67) In the Song of Deborah the tribes are listed in geographical groupings and it is improbable that Dan which is mentioned between Gad (Gilead) and Asher is an exception. Dan is listed next to Gad also in Gen 49 and Deut 33. The words אניות יגור למה (Ju 5 17) are difficult on any geographical location. From Ju 1 34 it is clear that Dan never reached the coast in the south. Hence the words above cannot be decisive. On this question v. Rowley, From Joseph to Joshua, 1948, pp. 81 sqq.

However, this whole conception of Ju 1 is based on a false premise: the Book of Joshua does *not* in fact relate *the conquest of all the cities of Canaan.*

Josh 10 contains no story about the conquest of Jerusalem and Gezer. Joshua defeats their kings but does not capture the cities. Similarly there is no story about the conquest of the five Philistine cities. In 11 22 we are explicitly told that Anakim remained in Gaza, Gath and Ashdod. In c. 11 only four cities are mentioned by name (1), the rest in the most general terms (2-3). For this reason, the picture is not clear. From v. 8 we learn, however, that Zidon Rabbah was not taken. In c. 12 (7-31) only thirty one kings are listed, some of them kings who were defeated but whose cities were not captured (Jerusalem, Gezer, Bethel, etc.). In this list there is no mention at all of Bethshean, Jibleam, Harosheth-hagoyyim, Jizreel, Acre, Tyre, Zidon, Laish, the Philistine cities, Ayalon, Shaalbim, Jaffa, and so on and so forth. Josh 13 1-6 describes the great national gap in the Conquest from Shihor to the Gateway to Hamath. In the Book of the Distribution (13-19) most of the gaps in the Conquest found in Ju 1 are specified. That Joshua did not complete the Conquest of Canaan within its borders as promised in Josh 1 3-4 is explicitly emphasized in cc. 13 and 23; assurance is even given that the Conquest will be completed after his death. We have already seen that the question of the completion of the Conquest troubled the historiosophers of that time. The only possibly misleading passages are the summaries in 10 40-42 and 11 16-23 which speak of the conquest of all the Land and the slaying of all its kings etc. But this is merely a certain terminological extravagance. For, in the exaggerated summary itself, at the end of c. 11, the incompleteness of the occupation at Gaza, Gath and Ashdod is mentioned (22). Exaggerated expressions are found elsewhere too in the book. At the close of the territorial list we are even told: "And Jahweh gave to Israel *all* the Land that he swore to give to their fathers" etc. (21 41), even though the list does not include the Lebanon and up to the Gateway to Hamath, nor even Dan's northern portion! This concluding phrase is alluded to in 23 14 beside the mention of "the remaining nations" who have still to be expelled. Clearly, the meaning of the summaries at the end of 10 and 11 is in fact just this — that by the wars of Joshua the question of the possession of Canaan *was decided* and that Joshua *seized* the Land and gave it into the possession of Israel. The author of Joshua was therefore able to introduce into the Book of Distribution passages from the same source as that from which Ju 1 is taken, even passages such as Josh 14 6-15 where Joshua himself blesses Caleb's intention to conquer Hebron, and Josh 17 14-18 where he urges on the Children of Joseph to conquer the Emeq. As if that were not enough, we are even told in 10-11 of *two* wars by Joshua himself against Hebron: after he had already put Hebron to the ban leaving no survivor (10 37), he again fought there (11 21-22). The great wars were followed by a series of mopping-up operations.

Furthermore, setting aside isolated expressions we have to bear in mind *the character of Joshua's wars* as described in Josh 1-11. They are wars of *destruction and extermination*, not of *occupation by immediate settlement*. Joshua does not leave garrisons in the cities which he has captured, but he returns with all the people to the camp at Gilgal. Only at the end of the war does he begin to distribute "lots". The reason will be discussed below. Here we merely note that the natural consequence of such wars was that Canaanite survivors fortified themselves in various places as best they could. Hence the tribes had to continue the fight when they started settling in their portions. In such a situation, a war by tribes was the inevitable second stage.

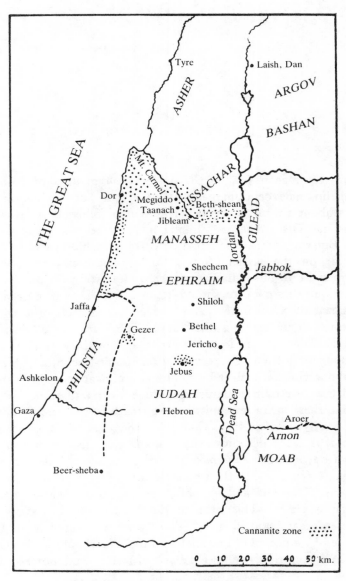

Canaanite cities in central Palestine
before the conquest of the Valley of Jizreel

JU 1 A CONTINUATION OF JOSH

For this reason Ju 1 is the perfect *continuation* of Josh and its heading unexceptionable. Ju 1 is a story of fragmentary excerpts about the *wars of the tribes* which followed on the wars of Joshua. The tribes are already in occupation each of its own "lot". But they were compelled by certain circumstances to renew the war on the *national* level. At a tribal assembly (such as described in Ju 20 18) it was resolved, following an oracle, that each tribe in its own lot should begin a fresh war to exterminate the surviving Canaanites. And indeed, in this chapter there is no story about *entering* the Land. The wars are all inside its borders. They are entirely different and distinct from those of the Book of Joshua. There is only one point of contact: Hebron. But about Hebron Josh itself contains no fewer than three stories. In all the rest of the material there is no parallelism.

That these wars are only an aftermath of the main Conquest is especially evident from the list of the *gaps in the Conquest* in Ju 1 21 27-35. This list shows us that, as early as the beginning of the period of Judges, *the bloc of real Israelite settlement* contains *amazingly few* gaps. In the territories of Judah, Simeon, Benjamin, Ephraim, Zebulun, and Naphtali there are no more than *six* Canaanite cities! This ethnographic situation necessarily presupposes great *national* wars. Thus what is related in Ju 1 was preceded by a period of national warfare. We should have to make such an assumption, even if the Book of Joshua were not extant.

MONUMENTAL EVIDENCE

This assumption is confirmed by several monumental facts.

1. In the period of Judges there is only *one* great Canaanite war: that of Barak and Deborah against Sisera (Ju 4-5). Even this war is fought on the northern border where a large national gap in the Conquest had been left. Scholars everywhere unearth "allusions" to the existence of Canaanite settlements within the Israelite territory. But against all the "allusions" stands a plain, evident fact, monumental as granite: Ju 5 *ends* the stretch of stories about the wars of Canaan. Ju 5 is a boundary stone. In the Pentateuch and Josh the Canaanites occupy the centre of the stage: they hold the Land, they are the enemy. In Ju 1 they are found only in certain places in the real Land of Israel. There is still an aftermath of internal Canaanite wars. After Ju 1 there are no more such wars. Instead, there begins the story of the wars against the enemies who *surround* the real Land of Israel. In 3 12-30 Moab, Ammon, Amalek make their appearance. In 3 31 we have the first mention of the Philistine. In 4-5 a great Canaanite war is fought out in the north, in an area marked as Canaanite in Ju 1. However, this is the *last* Canaanite war! After this war, the Canaanites never again apper as a military factor in the real Land of Israel. After Ju 5, begins the story of the wars against Midian, Amalek, Ammon, and especially the Philistines. There is no suggestion that the Philistines received support from a Canaanite element, hostile to Israel, living amongst the Israelite population. In the time of Saul and David, although there are still Canaanites at isolated points, this Canaanite element is no longer of any importance. The critics' stories about the Canaanite

"fortified zone", from Gibeon to Gezer, which cut the Land in two, and about the Canaanites' participation in the Philistine wars are fanciful legends, completely unwarranted by the sources. Saul's persecution of the Gibeonites, who were scattered throughout Israel, was due to religio-nationalist fanaticism (2 Sam 21 1-5). If the Gibeonites had been fighters and rebels, the whole story in 2 Sam 21 would not have been possible. Saul "forgot" Jebus and Gezer, because they were of no military importance. David conquered Jebus, because he wanted to establish his capital in a border-city which did not yet actually belong to any tribe. Gezer too he "forgot". Hivvite and Canaanite cities exist only on the northern border of his kingdom (2 Sam 24 7).

In the time of Solomon only a few Canaanite remnants are left in Israel, "all the remainder" of the Canaanites whom the Israelites could not put to the ban. These Solomon makes into slaves (1 Ki 9 20-21; cf. v. 22: "and of the Children of Israel Solomon did not make a slave"). Their descendants form a small class of "slaves of Solomon" which is mentioned in Ezr 2 55-57 Neh 7 57-59 11 3. This detail confutes the view that four of the twelve districts of Israel in Solomon's reign, which are listed in 1 Ki 4 7-19, are Canaanite — viz.: those mentioned in vv. 9-12 [68]. These four districts constitute a third of the whole country. Could Solomon have enslaved so numerous a people without a most serious upheaval? For, according to 1 Ki 9 20, Solomon enslaves *all* the remaining Canaanites". Moreover, on the view under discussion, Solomon naturalizes the Canaanites and gives their districts equal status with the Israelite districts, even relinquishing a certain administrative independence to them. Once more the question presents itself: if a third of the population was still Canaanite in Solomon's day, why is it never mentioned as a political factor either before Solomon or after him? How is it that they did not attempt to regain their freedom after Saul's defeat or at the time of the division of the Kingdom? The truth is that 1 Ki 4 contains no reference to the Canaanites. The twelve districts are explicitiy defined as divisions of *"all Israel"* (v. 7). It is incon-

---

68) Alt, Israels Gaue, pp. 12 sqq.

ceivable that four Canaanite units of population should be listed as four parts of "all Israel". One must recall that in 2 Sam 24 7 the Hivvite and Canaanite cities are separately and specially mentioned as such [69]. These four districts do, in fact, embrace the latest area of Israelite settlement, that which was formed after Dan's northward move and the conquest of the Emeq by Deborah and which certainly contained in part a mixed Israelite population (from various tribes). The vacuum left by Dan was filled by Benjamin, Judah and Joseph. A new, non-tribal unit came into being which formed Solomon's second district (v. 9). The third district is obviously of Manasseh: Aruboth and Socho are not mentioned as autonomous Canaanite cities, while Hepher is a clan of Manasseh. Likewise the fourth and fifth districts (11-12) undoubtedly belong to Manasseh, or mainly to Manasseh. Solomon split this region of Manasseh into three parts because of its

---

69) Those very critics who hold that four Canaanite districts were included in "Israel" at the same time maintain that Judah was not considered "Israelite" and therefore not included here, in spite of the fact that in all the chapters before and after c. 4 the obvious assumption is that Judah is an integral part of "Israel". The truth is, however, that the district of Judah is in fact included in the twelve districts. The country of Sihon and Og is erroneously listed twice: once, in v. 13 as Manasseh's territory in Transjordania and in v. 14 as the territory of Gad (and Reuben) — the area of "Mahanaim"; and a second time in v. 19, where the country of Sihon and Og is again mentioned. The name of the governor "Geber ben" in v. 19 resembles the name "ben Geber" in v. 13. V. 19 is undoubtedly a duplication of v. 13 which has been inserted here by mistake from a marginal gloss. The text should read: שמעי בן אלא בבנימין. ונציב אחד אשר בארץ יהודה. יהודה וישראל רבים וגו'. It is not to be supposed that Solomon exempted Judah from the King's maintenance, thus creating a source of envy and separatism. Nothing of the kind is mentioned in the story about the division of the Kingdom. Cf. Albright, Archaeology, p. 141. — It should be noted that Edom and the Philistine cities are not included in the list in c. 4. Presumably the King's maintenance was regarded as an obligation of honour which was imposed only on the Israelite population. For this reason too it is inconceivable that Canaanites should have been included in the list and Judah left out.

economic importance and its ability to support the king for three months. The cities mentioned in 9-12 are not cities of "sub-districts [70]. They were listed to delimit the new units which did not conform to the tribal portions [71].

Equally fictitious is the widely accepted scholarly fable, that *Shechem* was a Canaanite city in the time of *Gideon and Abimelech*. Abimelech's reign in Shechem follows on Gideon's rule with which he was invested by "the men of Israel" in recognition of his delivering them "from the hand of Midian" (Ju 8 22-23 9 1-2). The inhabitants of Shechem are included in "the men of Israel" whom Gideon saved from the power of Midian (9 16-19). Abimelech rules "over Israel" (ibid. 22) and he is one of those who arose "to deliver Israel" (10 1). In 9 28 there is apparently an obscure allusion to the remnants of enslaved Canaanites who still dwelt in the city. But Canaanites do not play any part in the story about the blood feuds of Abimelech's time. Shechem is not listed in Ju 1 amongst the Canaanite cities. — The disappearance of the Canaanites after Ju 5 is our first monumental fact.

2. The Israelites did not take over from the Canaanites the *military art* of the latter — their cavalry and iron chariots. The Israelite army is a force of swordsmen. David still does not know what to do with chariot horses, so he "houghs" them (2 Sam 8 4).

3. The Israelites did not take over from the Canaanites *their* political *regime* — the city-state. The Israelites are organized by

---

70) Alt, ibid, pp. 13, 15 et al.

71) The list in 1 Ki. 4 is basically *tribal* (as Alt recognized, ibid, pp. 12-13). It contains: Mount Ephraim (8), Manasseh's territory in Transjordania (13), Gad's territory (14), Naphtali, Asher, Issachar, Benjamin, Judah (15-19). Dan, being too small to maintain the King for a whole month, was presumably attached to Naphtali. Reuben was included in Gad, and Simeon in Judah, while Levi had no portion. Zebulun is not mentioned and we do not know where he lies hidden. Entirely new units are found only in Dan's ancient portion and in the western portion of Manasseh. This is a late, mixed, extremely prosperous region. These, and not its ethnographic peculiarity, are the characteristics which account for its special subdivisions.

tribes. The political system of Canaan was completely destroyed with the Israelite conquest. No Israelite, or Israelite-Canaanite, city-states were created. The Kingdom of Israel is *a completely new creation.* It arises from the will of the tribes for national unification. It appears as a politico-national *unity,* in contrast to the political separatism of the Canaanites. It was not preceded by local dynastic wars, nor is it the outcome of the victory of one dynasty over the others. It is a *united* state from the moment of its inception.

4. In the area of real Israelite settlement there are no Canaanite communites that exert an *idolatrous* influence upon Israel. In Josh 23 Israel was warned against the idolatrous influence of "the remaining nations" *round about* the real Land of Israel. In Josh 24 they were warned not to worship "the gods of the Amorite" who had been expelled from the Land (v. 12). The idolatrous influence came from "the peoples round about them" (Ju 2 12 3 3-6 10 6). So it is throughout the whole Bible. The Gibeonites of David's day are already worshippers of Jahweh (2 Sam 21 6 9). On the threshing floor of the Jebusite Araunah there is, to all appearances, no idolatrous symbol (ibid 24 21-25).

All these facts add up to a single monumental testimony that the Canaanite factor *had been liquidated* in the real Land of Israel as early as the beginning of the period of Judges. *At no stage* was the Conquest of the Land a process of peaceful settlement. It did not produce a national and cultural *intermingling.* The Canaanite element was *defeated and driven out.* This was possible only *by great national wars.* Herein is a decisive proof of the truthfulness of the narrative in the Book of Joshua.

THE REAL PLAN OF THE WARS OF CONQUEST

In the Book of Joshua the events of the Conquest are shrouded in a mist of legend. But through this legendary mist it is still possible to distinguish the actual march of events. When we examine this progress we see that the actions of Joshua are integral parts of a single *plan* which alone can explain to us, in terms of reality, the success of the Conquest.

The Canaanites had a most important technical-military advantage: they had a trained army with cavalry and chariots. The Israelite army consisted of popular levies, an army of sword-bearing infantry. But the Canaanites were disunited. In Canaan there was a centuries-old tradition of feuds between petty "kings". The population was a hotchpotch of peoples. The tribes of Israel could conquer them only by *unity*. This was an indispensable condition. In local and separate wars there would have been no hope of overcoming the Canaanites. The victory of the tribes proves that they fulfilled the condition: they fought as a united confederacy of tribes.

The unity of the tribes was not based upon any hard and fast political system. Its corner-stone was the religio-national covenant of the tribes made between them in the wilderness. It was symbolized, at that time, by *the prophetic leader* who stood at their head. The success of the Conquest therefore depended on that absolute submission to the leader's authority which alone could effectively restrain the separatism of the tribes. The stories about Joshua show that he was a leader and commander by the grace of God. All his deeds bear the stamp of an immensely dominating personality. He treasures above all two fundamentals: the *unity* of the tribes and their *"morale"*. He knows that the unity itself depends on morale. In addition, he has an instinctive appreciation of the objective military factors and knows how to use them.

At that time, the greatest danger threatening the unity of the tribes came from *their land-hunger*. They were land-starved and their objective in fighting was to gain possession of soil. There was a danger that they would, one by one, "cling" to the soil and their unity thus disintegrate. In each tribe the occupation of territory could have created the dangerous illusion that "its" war was now over. The first contact with the soil revealed this danger in stark colours: after the conquest of Transjordania two and a half tribes sought to secede from the covenant. This would have deprived the tribes of their great advantage over the Canaanites. It became essential to prevent "land-grabbing". This is why Joshua separates *the war* entirely from *the occupation of territory*. He keeps the people *in camp* for the whole duration of the war. No matter where the army fights, it always returns to the camp. Throughout the whole war Joshua does not occupy a single city, nor does he rebuild a single city. He only destroys and lays waste. He is compelled to prevent the people from occupying its portions until the end of the war, because he cannot be sure that he will be able to muster them for the general war if they are engaged in claiming land. This would appear to be the hidden reason for *the banning and cursing of Jericho*. This is a unique ban such as is neither mentioned nor paralleled in the Pentateuch. At the very moment when the people steps on to the soil of Canaan Joshua is forced to impress upon its mind the awareness that the war, at this stage, is not a war of occupation. He has to separate the war from the settling. The war is *a war for Jahweh*. Only after it has been concluded will the people receive a portion from Jahweh, "according to the word of Jahweh", by lot. So Joshua symbolizes the war's character by the total banning of the first city. The second city too, Ai, is turned by him into "an everlasting ruin". Thus does he drive it home that for the present he is not "giving" anything. This same necessity is the origin of the plan to distribute everything by "lot". And the terrible punishment meted out to Achan, who transgressed the ban, is certainly due to the same cause.

There was also another reason why Joshua had to keep the whole people in camp. Canaan contained no *central* royal city, the capture of which would have been decisive. There were tens of "centres". An actual occupation of the cities of Canaan, with the settlement of a population in them, would have involved leaving a garrison in each place. This would have dissipated the military strength of the tribes. It was easier to guard the women and children in a single camp, an arrangement which released most of the people for active service.

Joshua is especially careful to preserve the "morale" of the Israelite army. The tribes' greatest advantage lay in the *spirit* with which they were fired, the new *faith* for which they fought. This faith implanted in them their *absolute confidence in victory*, that confidence which is the source of every army's strength. Joshua works ceaselessly to increase this, drumming into the people by word and by deed the absolute confidence in victory. This explains his fondness for impressive *ceremonies*. In the stories, every action is follwed by ceremony. After the crossing of the Jordan he holds the ceremonial placing of the stones at Gilgal. After that, he circumcises those who came out of Egypt. Next, the Festival of freedom is celebrated. The conquest of Jericho is followed by the ceremonial cursing of Jericho. The conquest of Ai is followed by the ceremonial hanging of its king and the erection of a cairn over him. After this Joshua builds an altar on Mount Ebal and arranges a great festival. After defeating the confederacy of Southern Kings he performs the cruel ceremony of executing the five kings. The purpose of this ceremony is described as follows: "Be strong and of good courage, for thus shall Jahweh do to all your enemies" etc. (10 25). After the victory over the army of the Northern Kings, he performs, at Jahweh's command, the ceremony of houghing the horses and burning the chariots. The slight set-back before Ai is treated as a serious event by Joshua. The people *fled* and this is likely to undermine its absolute confidence in victory. So Joshua does not rest or relax until he has turned the very defeat into an additonal source of confidence. On receiving the news of the defeat he performs a ceremonial prayer of mourning. He sanctifies the people and brings the culprit to light by a divine trial. The

Judgment of Achan and his merciless execution together with all the members of his family constitute a most grimly impressive ceremony. The harsh punishment was essential to reinforce that absolute submission to the prophetic leader without which there was no hope of victory. Moreover, the discovery of the sinner and his punishment dispelled the *terror* inspired by the defeat. Indeed, the confidence, that God's hand was to be seen in everything that happened, was now strengthened.

Joshua's particular care to work upon the people's spirit by means of elaborate and detailed ceremoies can undoubtedly also be seen in the stories about the crossing of the Jordan and the capture of Jericho. These stories have a characther all of their own, unparalleld in the Bible. These wonders do not come to pass at the wave of a man of God's staff, but *through the whole people:* the Priests, or the Priests and the people, in their multitudes take part in the performance of the wonders; the Ark stands in the centre. The ceremonies are extremely complex, consisting of various actions, each done on a special word of command; different companies of the Priests and the people perform different roles which are fixed with precision. The people participates, but right up to the end it does not know exactly what will happen and it is on tip-toe with expectation [72]. There is no doubt that these

---

72) The large number of actions and orders, and the intricacy of the events, give the story in Josh 2-4 an appearance of heterogeneity. Hence it is not surprizing that Wellhausen and his school have tried by critical analysis to bre⸴k it up into several stories. But in fact the story is homogeneous. The proof is that *every* action, from its being ordered *to* its being performed, is related *only once :* 3 3-4, disposition of the people on the march ; 6, position of the Priests on the march ; 8, halting of the Priests at the edge of the Jordan ; 12, preparation of the Twelve ; 12-17, parting of the Jordan ; 4 1-8, taking out of the twelve stones ; 9, setting up of the stones in the Jordan ; 12-13, movement of the advance guard ; 15-18, ascent of the Priests and return of the water. Only in the *connecting verses* between the actions are there apparent duplications and inconsistencies. But these are no more than terminological inexactitudes and difficulties of sequence in the disposition of the material. Particular confusion has been caused by the ambiguity in meaning of the

legends have preserved the memory of actual ceremonial performances which fired the masses of the people. All this is most typical of Joshua. There is a personal "touch" about it all.

However, Joshua is not only a *leader* who understands the psychology of his people: the stories portray him also as a great *commander*.

Joshua picks on Gilgal as the site of the camp — an apparently strange choice. The supporters of the aetiological theory find in this a proof that these stories belong to the legendary tradition of the shrine at Gilgal. But in fact this choice of site suits a most objective conjunction of circumstances and it too bears

---

expression עבר לפני in 4 5 11. In 4 11 this expression is to be understood in the light of 3 6: the Priests *now moved from their position* in the Jordan, in order to *reach* their regular place "before the people". For, till then the people had been passing over while the Priests stood still; now the people stood still and waited for the Priests to pass over and reach the head of the column. In the continuation (12-13) we are told that the people did not actually go forward, but at that very moment the advance guard moved to take up its regular position in the order of the march. The Priests reach the edge of the Jordan's channel and wait for orders. These are given in 4 15-17. — 4 5 is to be understood in relation to the people's position at that moment. They were standing on the western bank, yet not *opposite* the Priests, but *to the side*. The Twelve had crossed with the people. So they had now to cross back diagonally and take up a position "before the ark of Jahweh". — Between 3 12 and 4 2-4 there is only a slight inconsistency of expression. Since the people crossed by tribes, Joshua had to choose the tribal representatives *before* the crossing, so that they could all stand ready on one spot. Hence 3 12 is in its proper place. We have only to understand that Joshua chooses the men without disclosing his purpose. The explanation comes only in 4 2-4. — In 4 10 the words ככל אשר צוה משה את יהושע are wanting in Septuagint variants and are undoubtedly a gloss. The words וימהרו העם ויעברו (ibid.) apparently refer to the Twelve and Joshua who still tarried in the Jordan and were the last of "the people". The beginning of v. 11 harks back to 4 1. — In 3 1-5 there is no chronological confusion, as Steuernagel maintains. וילינו in 3 3 does not mean precisely spending *one* night. מקצה שלשת ימים (2) means: at the close of the third day. This is consistent with מחר of v. 5.

witness that here a gifted historical *personality* is at work. There were several reasons for this choice. Joshua's wars were wars of destruction. Canaanite agriculture was ruined, and there was as yet no Israelite agriculture. Joshua had to get his supplies from somewhere. His supply base was Transjordania, in the territory of Gad, Reuben and half Manasseh. From Gilgal, close to Jericho, he could easily make contact with these tribes. Since he had booty in silver and gold, he could undoubtedly obtain supplies from Ammon and Moab too — an operation which, like the first, could be conveniently carried out from Gilgal. Its choice was, without doubt, also prompted by a twofold military consideration. It was only to be expected that Ammon and Moab would be hostile, seeing that the tribes had conquered (from Sihon, it is true) part of their country. The beginning of this enmity is related in the stories about Balak. And we know that Ammon and Moab subsequently fought bloody wars against Israel for hundreds of years. Even if they sold supplies for silver, they still remained a natural enemy. Since the Transjordanian tribes took part in the national war, their territory was exposed to attack. Thus it was essential "to keep an eye" on Ammon and Moab; and from Gilgal Joshua could bring speedy aid. The very proximity of the camp acted as a deterrent to hostile acts. Moreover, the existence of the camp in this place also served as a defence measure against a Moabite-Ammonite attack upon the rear of Joshua's own army. For all these reasons Joshua picked on Gilgal as the place for the "Jordan Guard" of the embattled people.

Again, the conduct of the wars bespeaks a commander's personality. Joshua does not fight *a single defensive war*. All his wars are *offensive*. He does not dig in in fortified positions: in all his encounters he employs field warfare. When he learns that an attack is impending, he anticipates it by an attack of his own. He exploits the factor of *surprize*. In a night march he climbs to the position of the kings besieging Gibeon and falls upon them *suddenly* (10 9). He also falls *suddenly* upon the kings in their gathering at the Waters of Merom (11 6). The flight of his own army before Ai is immediately exploited by him for a tactical purpose: he stages a decoy-rout. He makes consummate use of the topographical factor. The ambush is placed by him on the west of Ai, between Ai and Bethel. But he knows that the people of Bethel will come to the help of Ai. Now Ai lies south-east of Bethel and therefore a force from Bethel marching eastwards or southwards to Ai, would discover the ambush. For this reason Joshua draws up his army neither on the south nor on the east, but to the *north* of the city (8 11-13), so as to decoy the Bethel force northwards. This is certainly why he choses a position beyond *the valley* in front of Ai (ibid. 11), the object being to provoke the people of Bethel into a direct attack upon the Israelites and thus to deflect them from Ai, in which case they would have to cross the valley [73]. The rout of the Canaanites in the battle for Gibeon is exploited by Joshua with consummate skill. From his provisional camp near Maqqedah (10 21) [74] he sends units to harry the retreating enemy. He does not let his troops rest: the Canaanites must be prevented from reaching their cities (v. 19). He has time only to arrange the ceremonial hanging of the kings. But he does not permit the kings of Canaan a breathing space in which to reform their confederacy. In successive battles

---

73) The participation of Bethel thus explains the disposition of the army to the north and the words ובית אל in 8 17 are therefore not a "thoughtless" addition, as Steuernagel, Noth, and others maintain.

74) From v. 21 it is clear that Joshua at that time pitched a temporary camp in *Maqqedah*. On this basis v. 15 should be corrected to read: אל המחנה מקדה (instead of הגלגלה). The meaning of וַיָּשָׁב is here: came together after their return from the battles. V. 21 also contains the word וַיָּשֻׁבוּ. The reason for the scribe's error was that the permanent camp was at Gilgal and that after the battle they returned (as related in v. 43) to Gilgal. — V. 15 in the Massoretic text has greatly perplexed the critics, since it apparently rounds off the story in 1-14. Some delete it on the grounds that it is missing from Septuagint recensions. Of the critics who retain the verse, some consider vv. 16-27 as an additional story, an aetiological legend about the cave of Maqqedah. So Gressmann, Anfänge, p. 150 ; Elliger, PJB 1934, pp. 48 sqq : Rudolph, Elohist, p. 207. For a contrary view v. Wright, Problem, p. 110, n. 13. Rudolph indeed already sensed that vv. 18-21 do not suit an aetiological legend and he was therefore obliged to postulate a further story which has not remained extant. But the difficulty can be removed only by emending v. 15 from v. 21, as proposed above.

he defeats them one by one. In the war against the kings of the hill country he captures Libnah, Lachish and other cities in the Shephelah. It has already been stressed by Wright that this was also the strategy of Sennacherib and Nebuchadnezzar in their attack on Jerusalem. Here too, then, we see the true touch of a great commander.

THE COMPOSITION OF JOSH

The ancient Book of Joshua was presumably composed by a recorder of events at the beginning of the period of Judges, at the time of Dan's migration to the north. This author wrote in an ancient Deuteronomstic style. He collected the stories from living tradition and wrote them down in his own style This tradition was clothed in legends from the first. But it preserved the iron framework of the actual events. The author also possessed various written sources. He had "the Book of Jashar" before him. He had a list of portions, a list of boundaries and cities which also contained a list of the cities of Ephraim and Manasseh. But it is possible that he himself was a "chorographer" and that he himself wrote or completed the lists. He also had a *Priestly* scroll about the events of the Conquest and the Distribution of the Land, containing a list of the Priestly and Levitical cities. From this same scroll he excerpted chapters and passages for which he found a place in his own book; and something of its contents he worked into the war stories. He concluded the book with Joshua's dying instructions in 23 and with the story of his death and that of Elazar in 24 28-30 32 33. In a later edition Josh 24 1-27 was added. This chapter stands apart, for it alone contains the statement that in Joshua's time there were "foreign gods" in Israel (v. 23). It does not mention the gaps in the Conquest, nor Joshua's national testament. On the contrary, it assumes that the expulsion of the Canaanites has been completed (12 18). Only here do we find "the hornet" (12). In the rest of Josh there are wars, whereas in this chapter everything is done by "the hornet", without the use of sword and bow (ibid). The dispossession of the Canaanites takes the form of an *expulsion* (12 18) which is nowhere mentioned in the rest of the book. Nothing is said about the ban. This chapter is thus an addition. — In a still later Judahite edition the list of Ephraimite and Manassehite cities was omitted, and the boundary and city lists of the Galilean tribes were confused by abridgment. In this form the book has come down to us.